ALAMO

DEFENDERS

A Genealogy: The People and Their Words

By Bill Groneman

EAKIN PRESS ★ Austin, Texas

FIRST EDITION

Copyright © 1990
By Bill Groneman

Published in the United States of America
By Eakin Press
An Imprint of Eakin Publications, Inc.
P.O. Drawer 90159 ★ Austin, TX 78709-0159

ISBN 0-89015-757-X

Library of Congress Cataloging-in-Publication Data

Groneman, Bill.
   Alamo defenders : a genealogy, the people and their words / by Bill Groneman.
      p.   cm.
   ISBN 0-89015-757-X : $12.95
   1. Alamo (San Antonio, Tex.) — Siege, 1836 — Registers. 2. Alamo (San An-
tonio, Tex.) — Siege, 1836 — Biography. 3. Texas — Genealogy. 4. Soldiers —
Texas — San Antonio — Registers. 5. Registers of births, etc. — Texas. I. Title.
F390.G84   1990
976.4'03'0922 — dc20   89-29769
                                                                   CIP

For my parents,
Bill and Jean

*"Great spirits never
with their bodies die."*
— Robert Herrick

Contents

Acknowledgments

I would like to thank the following people for their help in the preparation of this book:

First and foremost, my wife Kelly, son Willy, and sheepdog Oreo for sharing our home with Alamo defenders for so many months; also friends, especially Bernice Strong, paragon of patience and archivist at the Daughters of the Republic of Texas Library at the Alamo; Steve Hardin of the Texas State Historical Association; Mike Boldt for his superb artwork; Kevin Young of San Antonio; Melissa Roberts for her fine job of editing; Cliff Choquette, the undisputed expert on Amos Pollard; Ray Esparza for sharing information on the Esparza family; and writers Walter Lord, for the information from his personal files, Curtis C. Davis, for directing me to his article on David Crockett, and Steven G. Kellman, for his information on Louis Rose. Thanks to Steve Beck, curator of the Alamo Museum; Marcia Evans and John W. Anderson of the Texas State Library and Archives; Bill Richter, Ralph L. Elder, and John Slate of the University of Texas at Austin; Bobby Santiesteban of the Texas General Land Office; Ruth Jarvis of the Tennessee State Library; Kay Bost of Southern Methodist University; George Ward, managing editor of the *Southwestern Historical Quarterly*; Dorothy Rapp, archives technician at the U.S. Military Academy at West Point; and members of the Alamo Society for their friendship and support. And also Thomas Ricks Lindley, whose painstaking search of Texas Archives and Land Office records continues to reveal new truths about the defenders of the Alamo.

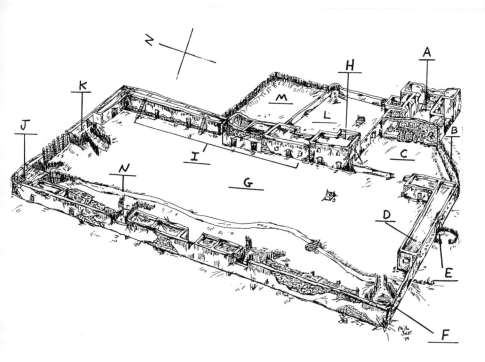

REFERENCE TO DIAGRAM OF THE ALAMO AS DRAWN BY MIKE BOLDT

A— Alamo Chapel: The Alamo's strongest building and the last position to fall during the battle. It was a place of dubious safety for most of the non-combatants since it also housed the garrison's gun powder supply. Major Robert Evans unsuccessfully tried to ignite the powder at the battle's end.

B— Wooden Pallisade: A makeshift barricade closing the gap between the Alamo Chapel and the Low Barracks. It consisted of two rows of wooden stakes with rocks and earth between. The outer row of stakes was higher than the inner row, with the earth and rocks serving as a firing step.

C— Inner Courtyard: This area was defended by Capt. Harrison's company. Mrs. Dickerson identified David Crockett's body in this area following the battle.

D— Low Barracks: James Bowie's quarters were located in this building. He died on his sick bed in a room just off the main entrance.

E— Main Entrance of the Alamo compound.

F— South West artillery position: Location of the Alamo's largest cannon, the 18-pounder.

G— The Main Plaza.

H— The Alamo's Hospital.

I— The Long Barracks.

J— North West artillery position.

K— North artillery position. Either this position, or the North West artillery position (J) was the site of William Barret Travis's death in the opening minutes of the battle.

L— Horse quartel.

M— Cattle pen.

N— Irrigation ditch.

Preface

"Where historic battles took place, and where historic people have lived, spirits linger."
— **Mardell Plainfeather**[1]

Perhaps historian Walter Lord stated it best when he wrote, "It is . . . a rash man indeed who claims he has the final answer to everything that happened at the Alamo."[2] It is true that no one knows the exact events surrounding the Alamo siege and battle, and it is also true that little is known of the people who made up the garrison of the Alamo.

We can be fairly sure of certain individuals who made up a solid corps of Alamo defenders. Their participation in the siege and battle can be verified through firsthand accounts, contemporary letters, muster rolls, and other official documents. But some individuals exist in a historical "gray" area. Their names are carried on lists of Alamo defenders, but very little is known about them or the role they actually played in the Alamo story. A little bit of documentation or evidence either way could establish them firmly as Alamo defenders forever, or quietly nudge them from the list.

There are still others who make up a sort of "waiting list" of Alamo heroes. Their names are linked with units which served at the Alamo or in San Antonio just before the siege, but the lack of really conclusive evidence has relegated these individuals to merely a "probable" or "possible" status as Alamo defenders.[3]

A list of Alamo casualties has existed from within weeks of the battle itself.[4] This list has been changed and altered over the years as new evidence concerning certain individuals has come to light. There is no reason to believe that the list, as presented in this book, will not be updated in the future as long as research into the subject continues.

Having one's name etched in stone is not even a guarantee of Alamo immortality. The name of at least one man on the monument in front of the Alamo was later found to have been put there in error. He had been considered a victim of the Alamo battle for years, until further research proved he had been murdered months before the battle took place.[5] By the same token, names which rightfully should have been on the monument and on the lists are only now being recognized.[6]

It is not the purpose of this work to establish a definitive roster of the Alamo garrison beyond all other investigation. The intent is to provide a listing of the generally recognized participants on the Texan side of the Alamo battle, with a few additions, from a biographical approach.

The people who were caught up in the battle of the Alamo were more than simply names on a list. To add a background, a description, or a human face to some of these names will, it is hoped, help in the appreciation of the Alamo as a human tragedy and a national event.

Of the hundreds of people who visit the Alamo every week, many still walk away wondering who the defenders of the Alamo really were, and what events brought together such a consistently heroic group. To answer that question, an individual has only to look around him at the scores of visitors inside the Alamo on any given day. He would not see professional warriors or mythological frontiersmen. He would see average people — the type who always come forth to fight their country's wars. Doctors, lawyers, teachers, farmers, merchants — these were the defenders of the Alamo.

When visitors to the Alamo stand in reverent silence before the names of the defenders of the Alamo, they are acknowledging their own kind. They are honoring people of different nationalities, religions, and races, from every walk of life, who made up the garrison of the Alamo for two short weeks in 1836.

These people and their actions on behalf of their country,

in many cases their adopted country, are the reasons we remember the Alamo. They were common people whose uncommon sacrifices elevated them to greatness in our collective memory.

The defenders of the Alamo were a diverse group of men, women, and children. Whether they were young or old, rich or poor, famous or unknown, they now share a special place in American history and in our memories. It is difficult to walk through the Alamo chapel today and not feel their presence. One can almost imagine them quietly mingling with the crowds of people visiting the Alamo every day.

One of the enduring legends of the battle of the Alamo, an event that produced no shortage of legends, is that the Alamo is still guarded by its garrison. It is easy to believe that their spirits linger there.

ADDENDUM

As research continues on the Battle of the Alamo, the roster of defenders is sure to be updated as new information comes to light. Recently, new information has been offered which suggests that James Hannum and Stephen Dennison did not die at the Alamo. According to this information, Hannum died of natural causes and was buried outside the walls of the La Bahia Mission at Goliad. Dennison's name is said to be carried on a list of those who were killed at Agua Dulce on 2 March 1836.

Also, continuing research may add the names of, A. Anderson, Conrad Eigenauer, I. L. K. Harrison, James Holloway, T. P. Hutchinson, John Morman, John Spratt to the official list, with the possibility of many others.

Traditionally, 183 has been given as the number of Alamo casualties. This number is solely based on the account of Francisco Antonio Ruiz, Alcalde of San Antonio de Bexar, at the time of the battle, who was charged with the disposal of the Texan bodies. Many past listings have conformed strictly to this number, despite other evidence which would indicate a greater number of defenders. Some accounts place the number as high as 250–260. In addition, at least one source indicates that as many as 1/4 of the Alamo's defenders may have died outside the walls, raising the possibility that they were not included in Ruiz's totals.

The role of John Sutherland, at the beginning of the Alamo siege has recently been called into question. There is documentation that places Sutherland in Bexar several days before the arrival of the Mexican troops. However, his own account of the events of 23 February 1836 are in variance with several other accounts, and a question has been raised as to whether he actually was in Bexar when the Alamo was besieged. Sutherland's role continues to be investigated, but there is not enough evidence, at this time, to exclude him from the list.

Part I

The People

"Where the ghosts of the Alamo gather again."
— Grantland Rice[1]

A word of explanation is necessary for the presentation of material in this list. The people listed include members of the Alamo garrison, whether they were killed, survived, or were sent out as couriers before the battle. Also included are noncombatant women and children who were present during the siege and battle. In the past, listings of Alamo heroes have included only the combatant casualties, with the survivors, couriers, and noncombatants relegated to little more than passing notice.

If known, the following information is given: age and occupation; place of birth; place of residence; military rank and utilization within the Alamo command; military unit to which the individual belonged; and whether or not the individual was killed in the Alamo battle (KIB).

The person's age refers to his or her age at the time of the battle (3/6/1836).

The place of residence refers to the last place at which the person lived, or where that person lived before the time of the siege and battle (2/23/1836–3/6/1836). In many cases this will be the person's home before immigrating to Texas, since

2

many individuals went directly into the field and did not have time to actually establish themselves as residents of Texas.

The defender's utilization, following his rank, indicates what function the individual fulfilled as a member of the garrison.

In regard to the military units of the defenders, it must be kept in mind that the Alamo garrison was not one unified military entity, but a combination of several smaller companies. Since these companies will be referred to throughout this work, some further description is necessary.

The nucleus of the Alamo garrison was under the command of Lt. Col. James C. Neill, left to occupy San Antonio de Bexar and the Alamo after the Texan army defeated the Mexican army and drove it from the town in December 1835.

Neill's command consisted of his staff, a small ordnance department under Maj. Robert Evans, an artillery company under Capt. William R. Carey (known as the Invincibles), and two small infantry companies known as the New Orleans Greys, under Capt. William Blazeby, and the Bexar Guards, under Capt. Robert White.

On 1/19/1836, Col. James Bowie reinforced the garrison with a company of volunteers under Capt. William C. M. Baker. Lt. Col. William B. Travis arrived in early February with a small cavalry company under Capt. John H. Forsyth. They were joined by another cavalry company under Capt. Juan N. Seguin. Two smaller groups of volunteers under Captains William H. Patton and Philip Dimitt also arrived, but the commanders did not remain in Bexar. Any of their men who did remain in Bexar were absorbed into other units. Capt. William B. Harrison arrived on or about 2/19/1836 with a small group of recent arrivals, the Tennessee Mounted Volunteers, from the United States.

The last group to reinforce the Alamo arrived on 3/1/1836, after the siege had progressed for eight days. This was a relief force from the town of Gonzales, made up of the town's militia force (the Gonzales Ranging Company of Mounted Volunteers), plus other residents of the town and surrounding area. Also, individuals who were already members of the Alamo garrison but had left Bexar for various reasons made up this last group.

ABAMILLO, JUAN (?–3/6/1836)
Born: Texas
Residence: Same
Rank: Sergeant (company noncommissioned officer; Capt.
  Juan N. Seguin's cavalry company)
KIB

Juan Abamillo was part of a company of twenty-four native Texans who enlisted for six months of service under the command of Capt. Juan N. Seguin. He took part in the siege and battle of Bexar (11/1/1835–12/9/1835).[2]

In 1873 and 1874, Seguin gave to Rueben M. Potter[3] a list of nine soldiers who, with him, were ten of the twenty-five men who accompanied Lt. Col. William Barret Travis to Bexar and the Alamo.

No land grants were ever cited for this defender for his service.

ALLEN, JAMES L. (1/2/1815–4/25/1901)
Age: 21 years (college student)
Born: Kentucky
Residence: Same
Rank: Private (rifleman/courier)
Left Alamo as a courier on 3/5/1836

James L. Allen was the oldest of seven children of Samuel and Mary Lamme Allen. His father was a veteran of the Indian wars, serving under Gen. William Henry Harrison.

James Allen was a student at Marion College when he joined other students to volunteer for military service in Texas. He was the last courier sent from the Alamo, leaving on 3/5/1836, the day before the battle took place.

He later served as a scout with Erastus "Deaf" Smith.[4] He missed participating in the actual battle of San Jacinto[5] but was instrumental in burning bridges behind Mexican lines, thus cutting off their means of retreat.

After the defeat of Santa Anna[6], Allen apparently returned to the United States and recruited volunteers for service in Texas. He returned to Texas as captain of a volunteer company, the Buckeye Rangers.

4

After settling in Texas, James Allen became a ranger in Captain Bell's company and fought in the Indian battle of Corpus Christi (July 1844).

He later settled in Indianola, dealing in the stock business and also serving, for a time, as mayor and justice of the peace.

In 1849 he married Frederica M. Manchan, and together they reared seven children.

At the outbreak of the Civil War, Allen was serving as the tax assessor/collector of Calhoun County, Texas. He was captured by Union troops but escaped to Port Lavaca.

In 1867 he moved to Hochein, Texas, where he owned a farm of 260 acres.

James Allen was a member of the Baptist church and a Mason. He was known for his hospitality and as being a substantial, progressive, and highly esteemed citizen.

He died at his home five miles west of Yoakum, Texas, on April 25, 1901.

ALLEN, ROBERT (?–3/6/1836)
Born: Virginia
Rank: Private (rifleman, Captain Forsyth's cavalry
  company)
KIB

Capt. John H. Forsyth, while on his way to Bexar and the Alamo, submitted a requisition to the provisional government of Texas for board for himself and six others. The name of R. Allen was given as one of these men.[7] Allen apparently continued on to the Alamo with Captain Forsyth's company.

This is the only verification that Allen was an Alamo soldier, since no bounty donation or headright certificates were ever filed in his name for his service to Texas.

Most lists of Alamo defenders give his name simply as "R. Allen."[8]

ALSBURY, JUANA NAVARRO DE (?–7/25/1898)
Residence: San Antonio de Bexar, Texas
Rank: Civilian (noncombatant)
Survived the Alamo battle

Juana Navarro de Alsbury was the daughter of José Angel Navarro II, who had been an officer in the Mexican army. She and her sister, Gertrudis Navarro, were the nieces of Vice-Governor Juan Martín Veramendi, James Bowie's father-in-law, and both girls were reared under the guardianship of Governor Veramendi and his wife.

Juana had originally been married to Alijo Perez. They had one son, Alijo Perez, Jr.

After the death of her husband, Juana married again. In January 1836 she married Dr. Horace Alsbury, a Texan soldier who had taken part in the siege and battle of Bexar. Dr. Alsbury was away from Bexar on a scouting mission when the Alamo siege began, on 2/23/1836, and Juana took refuge in the Alamo with her sister and infant son, probably under the protection of James Bowie.

On the morning of the Alamo battle, 3/6/1836, the two women and baby were sheltered in a room along the west wall of the mission-fortress. During the actual battle, Juana directed Gertrudis to open the door to the room to show the Mexican troops that only women and children were inside. When the Mexican soldiers saw her, they demanded that she give them her money and her husband. She told them that she had neither. The soldiers looted her trunk and clothes, taking what money they found.

A member of the garrison named Mitchell (either Napoleon B. Mitchell or Edwin T. Mitchell) tried to protect her but was bayonetted by the soldiers. A young Mexican defender tried to use her as a shield and was also bayonetted.[9]

After the Alamo battle, Juana was brought before Santa Anna, interviewed, and released.

In 1847 she was again widowed when Dr. Alsbury was killed in the Mexican War.

Juana later married Juan Perez, cousin of her first husband. In 1857 she received a pension from the State of Texas for her service at the Alamo. She died on 7/25/1898.

ANDROSS, MILES DeFOREST (1809–3/6/1836)
Age: 27 years
Born: Bradford, Vermont

Residence: San Patricio, Texas
Rank: Private (rifleman, Captain Blazeby's infantry
  company)
KIB

Miles D. Andross took part in the siege and battle of
Bexar. When Lt. Col. James C. Neill[10] left Bexar and passed
the command to Lieutenant Colonel Travis, he listed Andross
as "sick."

Most lists record his name as "Mills D. Andross."

AUTRY, MICAJAH (1794–3/6/1836)
Age: 42 years (farmer, teacher, lawyer, shopkeeper)
Born: Sampson County, North Carolina
Residence: Jackson, Tennessee
Rank: Private (rifleman, Capt. William B. Harrison's
  company, Volunteer Auxiliary Corps)[11]
KIB

Micajah Autry was the son of Theophilus and Elizabeth
Greer Autry.

During the War of 1812, he volunteered for service
against the British at age eighteen, marching to Wilmington,
North Carolina, as a member of Captain Lord's volunteer
company. At Charleston, South Carolina, he joined the
United States Army and remained in the service until 1815.

Due to bad health, possibly attributed to a war wound,
he was not able to continue farming and became a teacher. He
moved to Hayesboro, Tennessee, in 1823 and studied law.

In 1824 he married Martha Wyche Putny Wilkinson
(1796–1864), the widow of a Dr. Wilkinson. They had two
children, Mary and James L. Autry, and also reared a daughter by Martha's first marriage, Amelia.

In 1828 or 1829 Autry was admitted to the bar at Nashville. He practiced law in Jackson, Tennessee, from 1831 to
1835, in partnership with Andrew L. Martin.

Autry was a slaveholder in Tennessee. He started a mercantile business with his law partner, but was unsuccessful.

On business trips to New York and Philadelphia, he first
heard about the opportunities in Texas. In 1835 he left his

wife, children, and slaves in the care of Samuel Smith, his stepdaughter's husband, and set out for Texas.

On 12/7/1835 he booked passage on the steamboat *Pacific* in Nashville and traveled in the company of other men bound for Texas. By 12/13/1835 he was in Natchitoches, Louisiana, and one month later in Nacogdoches, Texas.

On 1/14/1836 Autry enlisted in the Volunteer Auxiliary Corps of Texas and set out for San Antonio de Bexar with David Crockett and others under the command of Capt. William B. Harrison. Their group would become popularly known as the Tennessee Mounted Volunteers. This company arrived in Bexar on or about 2/9/1836 and entered the Alamo with the rest of the garrison on 2/23/1836.

Micajah Autry was known as a sensitive man. He was an amateur poet, writer, artist, and musician. A letter of his, to his wife, dated 2/11/1834, is on display in the Alamo today.

Micajah's son James died in the Civil War, while serving as a colonel in the Confederate army.

BADILLO, JUAN ANTONIO (?–3/6/1836)
Born: Texas
Residence: Same
Rank: Sergeant (company NCO,[12] Captain Seguin's
  cavalry company)
KIB

Juan A. Badillo was one of the native Texans who enlisted for six months of service and fought in the siege and battle of Bexar under Capt. Juan N. Seguin. He accompanied Seguin back to Bexar and the Alamo in February 1836.

No land grants were ever cited for this defender.

His name is sometimes listed as "Antonio Padillo."

BAILEY, PETER JAMES III (1812–3/6/1836)
Age: 24 years (lawyer)
Born: Springfield, Logan County, Kentucky
Residence: Same
Rank: Private (rifleman, Captain Harrison's company,
  VAC)[13]
KIB

Peter J. Bailey III was the son of Gabriel and Sabra Rice Bailey. He was a graduate of Transylvania University, class of 1834.

In late 1835 he traveled to Texas with B. Archer M. Thomas, Daniel Cloud, William Fontleroy, and Joseph G. Washington.

He and his friends enlisted in the Volunteer Auxiliary Corps of Texas at Nacogdoches on 1/14/1836. They traveled to the Alamo with David Crockett as members of Captain Harrison's company.

Peter is mentioned in a letter written by Daniel Cloud to his brother on the way to the Alamo.[14]

His heirs received land in present Archer, Baylor, and Hamilton counties for his service. Bailey County, Texas, is named in his honor.

Peter's law degree from Transylvania University is in the holdings of the Daughters of the Republic of Texas Library at the Alamo.

BAKER, ISAAC G. (1804–3/6/1836)

Age: 32 years
Born: Arkansas
Residence: Gonzales, Texas
Rank: Private (rifleman, Gonzales Ranging Company of
   Mounted Volunteers)[15]
KIB

Isaac G. Baker arrived in DeWitt's Colony, Texas, on 8/13/1830. He received title to property in the town of Gonzales on 6/14/1832.

He joined the relief force under Capt. Albert Martin and Lt. George C. Kimbell, from the town of Gonzales, who went to the aid of the besieged defenders of the Alamo. He entered the Alamo with this group on 3/1/1836.

BAKER, WILLIAM CHARLES M. (?–3/6/1836)

Born: Missouri
Residence: Mississippi

Rank: Captain (company commander, probably the
commanding officer of the volunteers who accompanied
James Bowie back to Bexar and the Alamo)
KIB

William C. M. Baker came to Texas as a volunteer from
Mississippi, joining Captain Parrott's company of the Texan
army at Bexar on 11/26/1835. He took part in the siege and
battle of Bexar.

After Bexar was taken and the Texan forces reorganized,
he joined Captain Chenoweth's company on 1/1/1836.

It is possible that Baker left Bexar but returned within a
month as the captain of the men who accompanied James
Bowie to the Alamo.

BALLENTINE, JOHN J. (?–3/6/1836)
Born: Pennsylvania
Residence: Bastrop, Texas
Rank: Private (artilleryman, Captain Carey's artillery
company)
KIB

John J. Ballentine was a single man who lived in Bastrop
several years prior to 1836.

On some muster rolls or lists his name is shown as "Vol-
untine" or "J. Ballentine."

He is often confused with defender Richard W. Ballentine,
partly due to the fact that Alamo courier Benjamin F. Highsmith made an affidavit in 1895 stating that John J. and Richard W. were one and the same.[16]

It must be noted that when Highsmith made this affidavit, it was fifty-nine years after the Alamo's fall and he was
seventy-eight years old. Highsmith also stated that he was
well aquainted with all the soldiers in the Republic of Texas,
an exaggerated if not impossible claim.

BALLENTINE, RICHARD W. (1814–3/6/1836)
Age: 22 years
Born: Scotland

10

Residence: Alabama
Rank: Private (rifleman)
KIB

Richard W. Ballentine embarked for Texas on 12/9/1835 aboard the schooner *Santiago,* as did Alamo defender Cleveland K. Simmons.

His name is sometimes listed as "R. W. Valentine."

BAUGH, JOHN J. (1803–3/6/1836)
Age: 33 years
Born: Virginia
Residence: Same
Rank: Captain (adjutant staff officer)
KIB

John J. Baugh came to Texas as a first lieutenant of Captain Breece's 2nd company of New Orleans Greys and took part in the siege and battle of Bexar.

After the battle, he was promoted to captain and served as adjutant to the post at Bexar under Neill. He retained this position when the command of the Alamo forces went to Travis.

In his letter to Governor Henry Smith[17] of 2/13/1836, Baugh described the dispute between Travis and Bowie over command of the volunteer forces at Bexar. In the letter he generally favored the position of Travis in this matter.[18]

As Travis's adjutant, or executive officer, command of the Alamo would have gone to him after the death of Travis during the battle.

BAYLISS, JOSEPH (1808–3/6/1836)
Age: 28 years
Born: Tennessee
Residence: Same
Rank: Private (rifleman, Captain Harrison's company VAC)
KIB

Joseph Bayliss was a single man, and the son of John and Patience Bayliss.

11

Bayliss enlisted in the Volunteer Auxiliary Corps of Texas on 1/14/1836 at Nacogdoches, Texas. He joined the company of men under Captain Harrison and traveled to the Alamo with them.

His parents were his heirs.

BAYLOR, JOHN WALKER, JR. (December 1813–9/3/1836)
Age: 22 years (doctor)
Born: Woodlawn on Stone Creek, Bourbon Co., Kentucky
Residence: Fort Gibson, Arkansas
Rank: Private (rifleman/courier, Captain Dimitt's company)
Left Alamo as a courier, possibly on 2/25/1836

John W. Baylor, Jr., was the son of John W. and Sophia Maria Weidner Baylor. His father was a physician in the United States Army. His grandfather, Capt. Walker Baylor, was the commander of Gen. George Washington's Life Guard.

Baylor briefly attended Bardstown College in Kentucky before being appointed to the U.S. Military Academy at West Point. He enrolled on 7/1/1832 at Fort Gibson, Arkansas, under the name of Walker Baylor.

Intervention by President Andrew Jackson kept Baylor from being dismissed for disciplinary problems. He was, however, finally dismissed on 2/5/1833 for failing French. After his dismissal, he studied medicine for two years under his father. After the elder Baylor's death in January 1835, John Baylor left for Texas.

On 10/5/1835 he joined a group of volunteers under Capt. Philip Dimitt at Matagorda. Four days later he was in the town of Guadalupe Victoria as part of Captain Collingsworth's company, about to march on the town of Goliad. He signed an agreement with other members of the company, pledging protection to the citizens of Guadalupe Victoria. He took part in the capture of Goliad from Mexican troops on 10/9/1835.

On 11/21/1835 Baylor was part of a committee at Goliad assigned to prepare a preamble and resolutions expressing the volunteers' defiance of an order from Stephen F. Austin,[19] directing Captain Dimitt, whom the volunteers elected as their commander, to turn over control of the post to Captain Collingsworth.

On 10/28/1835 he took part in the battle of Concepcion[20] outside of Bexar. In November and early December, he took part in the siege and battle of Bexar.

By 12/20/1835 Baylor was back at Goliad and, along with other volunteers, signed a resolution pledging their lives, fortunes, and honor to establish Texas as a sovereign state.

He returned to Bexar and the Alamo with the small group under Philip Dimitt. During the course of the siege, he was utilized by Travis as a courier.

After leaving the Alamo, Baylor stayed in Goliad, serving in Colonel Fannin's[21] command with Capt. Jack Shackleford's Red Rovers and, later, Capt. Albert C. Horton's cavalry. When Fannin's retreating troops were caught in the open by a Mexican force, captured, and later executed, John Baylor was scouting ahead with the cavalry and missed the slaughter.

At the battle of San Jacinto he served in the 4th Company, 2nd Regiment of Texas Volunteers under Capt. William H. Patton.[22] He received a slight wound to his thigh during the battle.

In May and June of 1836, Baylor served with a group of Texas Rangers under Maj. Isaac Burton on the Texas coast. He took part in the seizure of three ships bound for the Mexican army with supplies.

On 7/25/1836 Baylor went on furlough from the Texan army and traveled to the home of his uncle, Robert Emmett Bledsoe Baylor, in Cahaba, Alabama. While there, he developed complications from his wound and died on 9/3/1836. His uncle came to Texas to settle Baylor's estate on behalf of his family.

John W. Baylor holds the distinction of having taken part in every major engagement of the Texas Revolution.

BLAIR, JOHN (1803–3/6/1836)
Age: 33 years
Born: Tennessee

Residence: Zavala's Colony, Texas
Rank: Private (rifleman, possibly Captain Baker's company)
KIB

On 2/19/1835 John Blair registered for one league of land twenty miles west of the town of Santa Anna in the vicinity of Wolf's Point.

Blair, a married man, may have been one of the volunteers who accompanied James Bowie to Bexar and the Alamo. Years later, Louis Rose testified that he "left him [John Blair] in the Alamo 3 March 1836."[23]

BLAIR, SAMUEL (1807–3/6/1836)
Age: 29 years
Born: Tennessee
Residence: McGloin's Colony, Texas
Rank: Captain (assistant to ordnance chief, Ordnance Dept.)
KIB

Samuel Blair was a single man. On 8/4/1834 he registered for one-quarter league of land in Power and Heweton's colony on the Agua Sarca Creek. On 9/10/1834 he registered for a headright of land in McGloin's colony.

Blair took part in the siege and battle of Bexar. He remained in Bexar after the battle, under the command of Lieutenant Colonel Neill. He served as assistant to the ordnance chief of the garrison and, as such, it would have been his duty to see to the maintenance of all the cannon and small arms of the Alamo.

BLAZEBY, WILLIAM (1795–3/6/1836)
Age: 41 years
Born: England
Residence: New York
Rank: Captain (commanding officer of infantry company)
KIB

William Blazeby came to Texas from New York, by way of New Orleans. He took part in the siege and battle of Bexar as a second lieutenant in Breece's company of New Orleans

Greys. He stayed in Bexar after the battle and was promoted to captain in the command of Lieutenant Colonel Neill.

During the siege and battle of the Alamo, Blazeby commanded his own infantry company, which was made up primarily of men who had been members of the New Orleans Greys. Although only part of the original, his company retained the identity of the Greys.

BONHAM, JAMES BUTLER (2/20/1807–3/6/1836)
Age: 29 years (lawyer)
Born: Edgefield County, South Carolina
Residence: Montgomery, Alabama
Rank: 2nd Lieutenant (courier/rifleman)
KIB

James B. Bonham was the son of James and Sophia Butler Smith Bonham.

He was expelled from South Carolina College in 1824 for leading a student protest against poor food and the obligation of students to go to class in bad weather.

He took up the study of law and began practicing in Pendleton, South Carolina, in 1830. In 1832 he served as an aid to Governor Hamilton during the Nullification Crisis, and commanded an artillery company in Charleston in case fighting broke out against the federal government.

Bonham was once sentenced to ninety days contempt of court in Pendleton for caning an opposing lawyer who insulted Bonham's female client, and for threatening to tweak the nose of the judge when he was ordered to apologize.

By April 1834 he had moved to Montgomery, Alabama, and set up his law practice.

In the fall of 1835, he went to Mobile and helped organize a volunteer company, the Mobile Greys, for service in Texas.

Bonham immigrated to Texas in November 1835 and immediately sought to establish himself in military and poltical affairs. In a letter to Sam Houston[24] of 12/1/1835, he offered to serve Texas without pay, lands, or rations.[25]

On 12/20/1835 he was commissioned a second lieutenant in the Texas cavalry. Within a week he set up his law practice in Brazoria. Although commissioned in the cavalry, he was never attached to any particular unit. He probably traveled to the Alamo with the volunteers under James Bowie, arriving on 1/19/1836.

Bonham immediately became involved in the political affairs of the garrison. On 1/26/1836 he was appointed one of a committee of seven to draft a preamble and resolutions on behalf of the garrison in support of Governor Henry Smith.

On 2/1/1836 he was an unsuccessful candidate in the election of delegates to represent the Bexar garrison at the Texas Constitutional Convention.

On or about 2/16/1836 Bonham was sent by Travis to obtain aid for the Alamo. He returned on 3/3/1836 with a letter from Maj. R. M. Williamson, a close friend and associate of Travis. The letter urged Travis to hold out, saying that help was on its way to the Alamo.[26]

Despite popular legend, it is very unlikely that Bonham and Travis were childhood companions in South Carolina. Recent evidence, however, indicates that they were second cousins.

James Bonham's role at the Alamo has been one of the most romanticized of all the defenders.

BOURNE, DANIEL (1810–3/6/1836)
Age: 26 years
Born: England
Residence: Gonzales, Texas
Rank: Private (artilleryman, Captain Carey's artillery
  company)
KIB

Daniel Bourne and his brothers immigrated to America from England. Daniel continued on to Texas and settled in Gonzales.

He took part in the siege and battle of Bexar as a member of Captain Parrott's artillery company. Following the battle, he stayed in Bexar as a member of Carey's company.

Bourne's brothers filed claims as his heirs. In 1858 they received a donation certificate for 640 acres of land in Palo Pinto County, Texas, and in 1862, a bounty warrant for another 1,920 acres. In 1861 they also received $250 for his military service.

BOWIE, JAMES (1795–3/6/1836)
Age: 40 years (sugar planter, slave trader, land speculator)
Born: probably Elliot Springs, Tennessee
Residence: San Antonio de Bexar, Texas
Rank: Colonel (commander of the volunteer troops among
   the Alamo garrison/co-commander of the garrison, 2/14/
   1836–2/24/1836)
KIB

James (Jim) Bowie was the son of Rezin and Elve Apcatesby Jones Bowie of Georgia. His father was a member of Francis Marion's (The Swamp Fox) dragoons during the Revolutionary War. He and his family lived in Tennessee, Missouri, and Kentucky before settling in Louisiana.

At age fifteen, Bowie left his family and settled on his own at Bayou Boeuf, Rapides Parish, Louisiana, and made a living sawing and selling lumber. He later operated a sugar plantation with his brother, Rezin P. Bowie, using the first steam-powered sugar mill in Louisiana. James also engaged in some shady business ventures, such as illegal slave trade with the pirate Jean Lafitte, and fraudulent land deals in Arkansas.

On 9/19/1827 Bowie took part in what would become known as the "Sand Bar Fight," a duel on a Mississippi sand bar just above Natchez, which erupted into a wild melee between the seconds and the supporters of the men involved. This incident, in which Bowie suffered several severe wounds, firmly established him as a legendary fighter throughout the South.

In 1828 James Bowie immigrated to Texas to pursue land dealings and settled in San Antonio de Bexar.

He met and courted Ursula Veramendi (1811–1833), the nineteen-year-old daughter of Juan Veramendi, the vice-governor of Coahuila-Texas. They were married in April 1831.

In November 1831, a new chapter was added to Bowie's legend when he and nine other companions fought off 160 Indians while searching for the legendary San Saba silver mines.

In September 1833, while Bowie was on a business trip to the United States, his wife and his in-laws tragically died in the cholera epidemic while in Monclova, Mexico.

At the outbreak of the Texas Revolution, Bowie never received a commission from the Texan government. He did, however, retain the title and authority of colonel, a rank that dated back to 1830, when he was elected as such in a Texas ranger company.

He took part in the battle of Concepcion on 10/28/1835, apparently sharing the command with James Walker Fannin.

Later, during the siege of Bexar, he served as aide-de-camp to Gen. Stephen F. Austin. When Austin left the field in order to solicit aid from the United States, in November of 1835, Bowie was an unsuccessful candidate to fill his position as commander of the volunteer forces besieging Bexar. He received less than one percent of the votes cast by the Texan soldiers.[27]

Later, at Goliad, he was named as leader of the ill-fated Matamoros Expedition by Sam Houston. This order was later rescinded.[28]

Bowie was directed by Houston to ride to Bexar with a company of men, apparently with orders to destroy the fortifications in the town and the Alamo, remove the cannons, and join the rest of the Texan army.[29]

When he arrived at Bexar on 1/19/1836, Bowie and Lieutenant Colonel Neill, commander of the garrison, determined that their position should and would be held, and Houston's directive was not carried out.[30]

On or about 2/12/1836 an election was held among the volunteers in the Bexar garrison in order to elect a volunteer officer as their commander.[31] James Bowie was elected, but in a strange episode he became extremely drunk and tried to assume authority over the town and the garrison.[32] Lt. Col. William B. Travis, who had been assigned to command by Neill in his absence, reached a workable agreement with Bowie on 2/14/1836, in which they would share overall command. Bowie would have authority over the volunteer troops, while Travis would command the regulars and the cavalry.

When the advanced guard of the Mexican army took possession of Bexar on 2/23/1836, the Texans fell back into the Alamo and Bowie dispatched Green Jameson with a message to the Mexicans, asking whether or not a parley had been requested. His message was rebuked and the Texans were informed that unconditional surrender was their only choice.

On 2/24/1836 Bowie became incapacitated by an ongoing illness, and full command of the garrison again fell to Travis.[33]

Bowie remained ill for the remainder of the siege and kept mostly to his quarters in one of the rooms of the low barracks, just east of the main gate of the Alamo. He was killed while lying in his bunk during the final assault on the Alamo.

James Bowie was described by his brother, John J. Bowie, as being about 6'1 and about 180 pounds. His eyes were dark, deepset, and gray-blue. His glance was calm but very penetrating. He had a very fair complexion and chestnut brown hair, and his hands were long and slender but very strong.

All contemporary descriptions portray Bowie as courteous, mannered, and polite. He was welcomed into upper-class society wherever he went, and was known as being kind and gentle in his dealings with men and absolutely courtly with women. Bowie was also described as being sincere, candid, and generous. He was a calm and mild man whose temper was terrible when aroused.[34]

Besides his service at the Alamo, James Bowie is best remembered for the use of the frontier knife invented by his brother, Rezin, which bears the Bowie name.

BOWMAN, JESSE B. (1785–3/6/1836)
Age: 51 years (hunter, trapper)
Born: Tennessee
Residence: Red River County, Texas
Rank: Private (rifleman)
KIB

Jesse B. Bowman was born in Tennessee, but by 1811 he lived in Illinois, where his son, Joseph T. Bowman, was born.

In 1824 he moved to Arkansas and became the first known settler of Camden in Ouachita County, where he lived with his wife and three children. By 1828 he had moved to Hempstead, Arkansas.

In the 1830s, Bowman, along with his son Joseph, his brother, and nephews, came to Texas. He received land in Red River County.

He and his son both served in the Texan army during the Texas Revolution. Jesse Bowman became part of the Alamo garrison and died in the battle on 3/6/1836.

BROWN, GEORGE (1801–3/6/1836)
Age: 35 years
Born: England
Residence: Gonzales, Texas
Rank: Private (rifleman)
KIB

George Brown came to Texas from Yazoo, Mississippi.

He was one of four "George Browns" in the Texan army at the time. His name is given on muster rolls simply as "Brown."

BROWN, JAMES (1800–3/6/1836)
Age: 36 years
Born: Pennsylvania
Residence: DeLeon's Colony, Texas
Rank: Private (rifleman)
KIB

James Brown came to Texas from Pennsylvania in 1835. He registered in DeLeon's Colony on 4/17/1835.

He took part in the siege and battle of Bexar.

His name is usually listed simply as "Brown" on muster rolls.

BROWN, ROBERT (1818?–?)
-Age: possibly 18 years
Residence: Texas
Rank: Private (rifleman/raider/courier)
Left Alamo as a courier

Robert Brown arrived in Texas in October 1835. He was a single man.

Brown is mentioned by Travis, in his letter of 2/25/1836, as being one of the men who sallied forth from the Alamo to burn huts in La Villita, which were affording cover to the Mexican troops.[35]

He was apparently sent out of the Alamo as a courier sometime after 2/25/1836.

During the San Jacinto campaign, he rendered service by guarding baggage at the town of Harrisburg, Texas.

BUCHANAN, JAMES (1813–3/6/1836)
Age: 23 years
Born: Alabama
Residence: Austin's Colony, Texas
Rank: Private (rifleman)
KIB

James Buchanan and his wife, Mary, registered in Austin's Colony in 1834.

His heirs received a bounty land grant for his death at the Alamo.

BURNS, SAMUEL E. (1810–3/6/1836)
Age: 26 years
Born: Ireland
Residence: Natchitoches, Louisiana
Rank: Private (artilleryman, Captain Carey's artillery company)
KIB

On most lists of Alamo victims he is listed merely as "Burns."

BUTLER, GEORGE D. (1813–3/6/1836)
Age: 23 years
Born: Missouri
Rank: Private (rifleman)
KIB

George D. Butler came to Texas by way of New Orleans.

CAIN, JOHN (1802–3/6/1836)
Age: 34 years
Born: Pennsylvania
Residence: Gonzales, Texas
Rank: Private (artilleryman, Captain Carey's artillery
  company)
KIB

John Cain took part in the siege and battle of Bexar and
was issued a donation certificate for 640 acres for his service.
He remained in Bexar as an artilleryman in Carey's company.

Sometime before the siege of the Alamo began, he returned to his home in Gonzales, but came back to the Alamo
on 3/1/1836 with the relief force from Gonzales.

His name is sometimes listed as "Cane."

CAMPBELL, ROBERT (1810–3/6/1836)
Age: 26 years
Born: Tennessee
Residence: Same
Rank: Lieutenant (company officer, Captain Harrison's
  company, VAC)
KIB

Robert Campbell came to Texas in January 1836.

The only evidence of his having fought and died at the
Alamo is a document by Col. Sidney Sherman of the 2nd Regiment of Texas Volunteers, dated 4/24/1836. This document
involves the claim of Lt. A. L. Harrison for the price of his
horse and gun in the service of Texas. Harrison stated that his
property was appraised by "Capt. W. B. Harrison, Col.
Crockett and Lieut. Robert Campbell," and that, "all these
appraisers fell in the defense of the Alamo . . ."[36]

CAREY, WILLIAM R. (1806–3/6/1836)
Age: 30 years
Born: Virginia
Residence: Washington-on-the-Brazos, Texas
Rank: Captain (commanding officer of artillery company)
KIB

William R. Carey was the son of Moses Carey of Virginia. He was a single man when he came to Texas from New Orleans, arriving at Washington-on-the-Brazos on 7/28/1835.

When the Texas Revolution broke out, he joined the Volunteer Army of Texas and was among the troops who marched to the town of Gonzales during the fight for the Gonzales cannon.[37] He was appointed second lieutenant on 10/28/1835.

During the siege and battle of Bexar, Carey received a slight wound to the scalp while manning a cannon. He was promoted to first lieutenant in the field for his actions in the battle.

On 12/14/1835 he was elected captain by popular vote of his fifty-six-man artillery company, which he called "The Invincibles." This company remained in Bexar as part of the garrison under Lieutenant Colonel Neill, with Carey as its commanding officer. At this time, Carey actually commanded the Alamo and the troops stationed there, while Neill commanded Bexar and the troops in town.

Carey's artillerymen were utilized by Neill as "trouble shooters" for any tough task at hand, even acting as military police.[38] During the siege and battle of the Alamo, Carey commanded the fort's artillery.

His father was his heir and traveled to Texas to settle his estate. He received $198.65 for his son's military service.

According to a document filed by his father, it is possible that a "private servant" (a slave) died with William Carey at the Alamo.[39]

CLARK, CHARLES HENRY (?–3/6/1836)
Born: Missouri
Residence: Same
Rank: Private (rifleman)
KIB

Charles H. Clark, a single man, came to Texas in November 1835 as a member of Captain Breece's company of New Orleans Greys. He took part in the siege and battle of Bexar.

His nephew was his heir.

CLARK, M. B. (?–3/6/1836)
Born: Mississippi
Rank: Private (rifleman, possibly Captain Baker's company)
KIB

M. B. Clark joined the company of Captain Chenoweth on 1/27/1836. He may have been one of the volunteers who accompanied James Bowie back to Bexar and the Alamo.
Louis Rose stated he ". . . saw him a few days before the fall of the Alamo."[40]

CLOUD, DANIEL W. (2/20/1812–3/6/1836)
Age: 24 years (lawyer)
Born: Lexington, Kentucky
Residence: Logan County, Kentucky
Rank: Private (rifleman, Captain Harrison's company, VAC)
KIB

Daniel W. Cloud was the son of Daniel and Nancy Owen Cloud. He traveled through Illinois, Missouri, Arkansas, and Louisiana before going to Texas. He went to Texas with B. Archer, M. Thomas, Peter J. Bailey, William Fontleroy, and Joseph G. Washington.
Cloud enlisted in the Volunteer Auxiliary Corps of Texas on 1/14/1836 at Nacogdoches, before Judge Forbes. He joined Captain Harrison's company and traveled to Bexar and the Alamo with this group.

COCHRAN, ROBERT E. (1810–3/6/1836)
Age: 26 years
Born: New Jersey
Residence: Brazoria, Texas
Rank: Private (artilleryman, Captain Carey's artillery company)
KIB

Robert E. Cochran probably lived in Boston and then New Orleans before 1834. For a time, he conducted business with Ammon Underwood. He came to Texas in 1835 and settled in Brazoria.

He took part in the siege and battle of Bexar and remained in Bexar as a member of Carey's company.

Cochran County, Texas, created from Bexar County, is named in his honor.

COTTLE, GEORGE WASHINGTON (1811–3/6/1836)
Age: 25 years
Born: Hurricane Township, Lincoln County, Missouri
Residence: DeWitt's Colony, Texas
Gonzales Ranging Company
KIB

George W. Cottle was the son of Jonathan and Margaret Cottle of Missouri. He came to DeWitt's Colony, Texas, with his family on 7/6/1829.

Cottle married his cousin, Eliza, on 11/7/1830, but the marriage was annulled eleven months later.

On 9/12/1835 he was granted title to one league of land on the Tejocotes Creek and La Vaca River, twenty-eight miles from Gonzales.

He married a second time, on 1/4/1835, to Nancy Curtis Oliver. They had one daughter, Melvinia.

During the fight for the Gonzales cannon, in late September of 1835, George Cottle served as a courier to rally reinforcements to Gonzales. He fought in the actual skirmish for the cannon, on 10/2/1835, in which the Mexican force was driven back toward Bexar.

Cottle went to the Alamo as part of the relief force from Gonzales, arriving there on 3/1/1836.

His brother-in-law, Thomas J. Jackson, also died at the Alamo.

COURTMAN, HENRY (1808–3/6/1836)
Age: 28 years
Born: Germany
Residence: Same
Rank: Private (rifleman)
KIB

Henry Courtman came to Texas, by way of New Orleans, as a member of Breece's New Orleans Greys. He took part in the siege and battle of Bexar, and remained in Bexar, probably as a member of Blazeby's company.

His brother, George F. Courtman, died in the Goliad massacre.[41]

CRAWFORD, LEMUEL (1814–3/6/1836)
Age: 22 years
Born: South Carolina
Residence: Same
Rank: Private (artilleryman, Captain Carey's artillery
  company)
KIB

Lemuel Crawford enlisted in the service of Texas in early October of 1835 and served until December 26 as an artilleryman. He probably took part in the siege and battle of Bexar.

He remained in Bexar and reenlisted on 2/13/1836, serving in the Alamo garrison as a member of Carey's company.

CROCKETT, DAVID (8/17/1786–3/6/1836)
Age: 49 years (former United States congressman)
Born: Green County, Tennessee
Residence: Weakley County, Tennessee
Rank: Private (rifleman, Captain Harrison's company,
  VAC)
KIB

David Crockett was the son of John and Rebecca Hawkins Crockett. As a twelve-year-old boy, with no education, he left home on a cattle drive to Virginia, and remained away from home for two years, traveling to various points in the East.

On 8/12/1806 Crockett married Polly Finley. They had two sons and a daughter and lived in Lincoln County, Tennessee. Crockett farmed there, but usually sustained his family through his hunting skills.

In 1813 he enlisted in a militia unit in Winchester, Tennessee, to serve in the Creek Indian War. He took part in the massacre of Indians at Tallusahatchee, and later served in pursuit of Indians through the Florida swamps. He resigned with the rank of sergeant after serving two hitches with the army.

Crockett's wife died in 1815, but he soon married again. His second wife was Elizabeth Patton, a widow with two children whose husband was killed in the Creek War. Crockett and she had a son and daughter and he reared her children as his own.

The Crockett family moved further west in Tennessee, where David became involved in local politics and government. He served as magistrate for the Shoal Creek community and was also elected colonel of the local militia unit. He was also involved in various business ventures without too much success. He attempted to transport barrel staves down the Mississippi River by flatboat, but his trip ended in disaster when the boats sank and he was almost drowned. A grist mill, powder mill, and distillery that he owned met a similar fate when it was washed away in a flood.

In 1821 and 1823, Crockett was elected to the Tennessee legislature, representing a district of eleven western counties of the state.

He later served in the United States Congress, representing Tennessee for the periods 1827–1831 and 1833–1835. His congressional record was unspectacular, and he was known for missing many roll calls. His pet projects were squatters' rights and the prevention of uprooting the Cherokee and other southeastern Indian tribes from their traditional lands.

His stands brought him into conflict with President Andrew Jackson, and his outspoken opposition to the president ultimately led to Crockett's political defeat in 1835. Ironically, he is credited as being one of those who subdued a man attempting to assassinate Jackson in 1835.

Following his electoral defeat in 1835, David Crockett decided to search out new lands and opportunities in Texas. He traveled from Tennessee to Texas with a small group of friends, none of whom would continue on with him to the Alamo.

On 1/14/1836 David was sworn into the Volunteer Auxiliary Corps of Texas at Nacogdoches and became a member of Capt. William Harrison's company. He traveled to Bexar and the Alamo with this group, arriving on or about 2/9/1836.

When the Mexican army appeared at Bexar on 2/23/1836, Harrison's company, along with David, was assigned the job of guarding the town while the rest of the garrison fell back to the Alamo.[42]

Crockett accompanied the injured Dr. John Sutherland into the Alamo, to Travis. According to Sutherland, Crockett asked Travis which area he and his companions should defend. Travis assigned to them the low wooden palisade which ran from the Alamo chapel to the low barracks of the south wall.[43]

David Crockett did not have any rank other than private at the Alamo, and he did not figure into the chain of command. He was, however, sometimes referred to as "Colonel," which was a title of respect rather than authority, dating back to his days in the Tennessee militia.

During the course of the siege, Crockett's actions were praised in a letter by Travis, who wrote, "The Hon. David Crockett was seen at all points, animating the men to do their duty."[44] An enduring story of the Alamo describes Crockett playing a fiddle accompanied by John McGregor on the bagpipes to boost the spirits of the members of the garrison.

David Crockett died during the battle of the Alamo while defending his assigned area in front of the chapel. Susannah Dickerson remembered seeing his body between the chapel and the two-story hospital building, while being led from the scene.[45]

Crockett is described as having been extremely generous. He was known to have freely shared the meat from his hunts, and his cabin door was said to be always open. He had a relaxed and carefree attitude and was never hesitant about leaving his family to embark on some new trip.

Contemporary accounts describe David as not being coarse in speech or manner. He did not use profanity, and his stories were marked with "an earnestness of truth."[46] He is also described as being pleasant, courteous, and an interesting man of fine instincts and intellect.

Crockett had a very good sense of humor, and although he had a very minimal education, his speech was not dependent upon backwoods expressions. However, he did know how to use them to help make a point.

As a congressman, Crockett was a sincere legislator who could not be swayed from his beliefs. But he was somewhat naive and was used by others toward their own political ends.

Several portraits of David Crockett exist or have existed. The portraits which have survived to this day are consistent in certain features. They show him to be a good-looking man with bright eyes, a long hawklike nose, high cheek bones, ruddy cheeks, and a large and firm chin.[47] The one full-length portrait shows him to be of average height with a solid build.[48]

David Crockett was without a doubt the most famous defender of the Alamo, and was nationally known during his lifetime. Accordingly, his life and role in the Alamo battle have inspired more myths and legends than those of any other defender.

CROSSMAN, ROBERT (1810–3/6/1836)
Age: 26 years
Born: Pennsylvania
Residence: Same
Rank: Private (rifleman, Captain Blazeby's infantry
  company)
KIB

Robert Crossman was the son of Ebeneser Crossman. He immigrated to Texas by way of New Orleans as a member of Breece's company of New Orleans Greys.

Crossman took part in and was wounded in the siege and battle of Bexar. He remained in Bexar as a member of Blazeby's company.

His name is often misspelled on muster rolls as "Crosson" or "Crasson."

CRUZ Y AROCHA, ANTONIO
Born: Mexico
Residence: Same
Rank: Private (Captain Seguin's orderly/courier, Captain
  Seguin's cavalry company)
Left Alamo as a courier on 2/25/1836

Antonio Cruz y Arocha was one of Seguin's company of native Texans, recruited for six months of service.

He took part in the siege and battle of Bexar and returned to Bexar and the Alamo with Seguin and Travis. He left the Alamo on 2/25/1836 as a courier, accompanying Seguin on his mission to rally reinforcements for the Alamo.

He later served in Seguin's company in the battle of San Jacinto.

CUMMINGS, DAVID P. (1809–3/6/1836)
Age: 27 years (surveyor)
Born: Lewiston, Pennsylvania
Residence: Pennsylvania
Rank: Private (rifleman)
KIB

David Cummings was the son of David and Elizabeth Cathers Cummings. His father was a successful Harrisburg canal man and an aquaintance of Sam Houston.

Cummings traveled by boat from New Orleans, arriving in Texas in mid-December of 1835. He proceeded on foot to San Felipe, where he sold his best rifle for $30. He met Sam Houston and presented to him a letter of introduction from his father. Houston advised him to obtain a horse and proceed to Goliad, where they would meet later.

Cummings wanted to join a ranger company to protect the frontier from Indians. He traveled to Gonzales and then Bexar, where he joined the garrison in late January or early February 1836.

David left Bexar sometime after 2/14/1836, to survey lands entitled to him on the Cibolo Creek. He was picked up by the Gonzales relief force on their way to Bexar and entered the Alamo with them on 3/1/1836.

David Cummings was a cousin to Alamo defender John Purdy Reynolds by marriage.

CUNNINGHAM, ROBERT (10/18/1804–3/6/1836)
Age: 31 years (flatboatman)

Born: Ontario County, New York
Residence: Skull Creek, Austin's Colony, Texas
Rank: Private (artilleryman, Captain Carey's artillery
  company)
KIB

Robert Cunningham was the oldest of seven children of David and Anna Jennison Cunningham. He lived with his family in Laugehery Creek, Indiana; Louisville, Kentucky; and Jeffersonville, Indiana before immigrating to Texas.

In 1832 he worked on a cargo flatboat to New Orleans. From there he wrote to his family, telling them he would be staying in New Orleans. By 3/4/1833 he was in Texas, where he received title to one league of land in Austin's Colony.

His family next heard from him in 1835, when he wrote and told them he had moved to Texas and joined the Texan army.

Cunningham took part in the siege and battle of Bexar as a sergeant and second gunner in Capt. T. L. F. Parrott's artillery company. He stayed in Bexar after it was taken and served as a private in Carey's artillery company.

Robert Cunningham was a single man, and his mother was his heir. She was awarded land bounties of 3255.36 acres in Bell County, 640 acres in Parker County, and 138 acres in Coryell County, for her son's service and death in the Texas Revolution.

DARST, JACOB C. (12/22/1793–3/6/1836)
Age: 42 years (farmer)
Born: Woodford County, Kentucky
Residence: Gonzales, Texas
Rank: Private (rifleman, Gonzales Ranging Company)
KIB

Jacob C. Darst was the son of David and Rosetta Holman Darst. He married Elizabeth Bryan (1796–1820) on 3/25/1813 in Charles County, Missouri. After the death of his wife he married Margaret C. Hughes, in 1820.

He, his wife, and two children left their Missouri farm for Texas in 1830, arriving in DeWitt's Colony on 1/10/1831.

On 4/24/1831 he registered for twenty-four labors of land on the Guadalupe River above Gonzales. In July of that year he also registered for one labor of land on a creek which emptied into the LaVaca Creek.

Darst was one of the "Old Eighteen," original defenders of the Gonzales cannon in late September 1835. He was mustered into service in the Gonzales Ranging Company on 2/23/1836. On 3/1/1836 he entered the Alamo with this unit.

His name is sometimes listed as "Durst" or "Dust."

DAVIS, JOHN (1811–3/6/1836)
Age: 25 years
Born: Kentucky
Residence: Gonzales, Texas
Rank: Private (rifleman, Gonzales Ranging Company)
KIB

John Davis left Kentucky while in his late teens. His twin brother remained behind when he moved to Texas.

He received title to one-quarter league of land on the LaVaca Creek in DeWitt's Colony on 10/28/1831.

In Texas, Davis gained a reputation for his actions in engagements with Indians.

On 2/23/1836 he was mustered into service as a member of the Gonzales Ranging Company. He entered the Alamo with this unit on 3/1/1836.

DAY, FREEMAN H. K. (1806–3/6/1836)
Age: 30 years
Rank: Private (rifleman, Captain White's infantry company)
KIB

Freeman H. K. Day took part in the siege and battle of Bexar and remained in Bexar afterwards as an infantryman in the Bexar Guards.

He received a donation certificate for 640 acres of land for his part in the siege of Bexar.

DAY, JERRY C. (1816–3/6/1836)
Age: 20 years

Born: Missouri
Residence: near Gonzales, Texas
Rank: Private (rifleman)
KIB

Jerry C. Day was the son of Jeremiah Day, who served the Texan forces from 1836 to 1838 as a wagoner.

DAYMON, SQUIRE (1808–3/6/1836)
Age: 28 years
Born: Tennessee
Residence: Gonzales, Texas
Rank: Private (artilleryman, Captain Carey's artillery
    company)
KIB

Squire Daymon took part in the siege and battle of Bexar. He remained in Bexar as a member of Carey's company.

Sometime after 2/2/1836, he left Bexar and went to his home in Gonzales. He returned to Bexar and the Alamo along with the relief force from the town of Gonzales on 3/1/1836.

DEARDUFF, WILLIAM (?–3/6/1836)
Born: Tennessee
Residence: Gonzales, Texas
Rank: Private (rifleman)

William Dearduff immigrated to Texas from Tennessee. He registered for one-quarter league of land in DeWitt's Colony on 11/5/1831.

He entered the Alamo on 3/1/1836 with the relief force from Gonzales.

Dearduff was the brother-in-law of Alamo defender James George.

DE LA GARZA, ALEXANDRO
Born: Texas
Residence: Same
Rank: Private (rifleman/courier, Captain Seguin's cavalry
    company)
Left Alamo as a courier (date unknown)

Alexandro de la Garza was one of the company of native Texans recruited by Juan Seguin for six months of service. He took part in the siege and battle of Bexar and returned to Bexar with Seguin and Travis in early February 1836.

In later life, Juan Seguin stated that Alexandro was sent from the Alamo as a courier.

DENNISON, STEPHEN (1812–3/6/1836)
Age: 24 years (glazer, painter)
Born: England or Ireland
Residence: Kentucky
Rank: Private (rifleman, Captain Blazeby's infantry
 company)
KIB

Stephen Dennison came to Texas by way of New Orleans as a member of Breece's New Orleans Greys.

He took part in the siege and battle of Bexar and remained in Bexar as a member of Blazeby's company.

After Dennison's death at the Alamo, H. F. Smith of Louisville, Kentucky, presented a headright claim in Texas in Dennison's name.

DeSAUQUE, FRANCIS L. (?–3/27/1836)
Merchant, store owner
Born: Philadelphia, Pennsylvania
Residence: Matagorda, Texas
Rank: Captain (courier, probably Captain Dimitt's
 company)
Left Bexar on or about 2/22/1836 to obtain provisions for the
 garrison

Francis L. DeSauque, a married man, came to Texas in 1835, settling in Matagorda County on one league and labor of land.

He entered the service of Texas on 10/10/1835.

DeSauque came to Bexar sometime before the siege of the Alamo began, probably along with Capt. Philip Dimitt. He was sent out from Bexar shortly before the arrival of the Mexican army in order to obtain supplies. While in Bexar he loaned Travis $200 for the garrison, charged against the account of the Texan government.

DeSauque made his way to Goliad and Fannin's command, and brought news of the Alamo's need for supplies.

He was with Captain Chenoweth, returning to Bexar with supplies, when he received a letter from Fannin. The letter described the colonel's abortive attempt to reach the Alamo and advised DeSauque to return to Goliad or try to reach Gonzales and confer with the officers there.[49]

He returned to Fannin's command and was taken prisoner, along with this group, by the Mexican army on 3/20/1836. He was executed one week later in the mass murder of the bulk of Fannin's command.

DeSauque's heirs received 1,920 acres of land for his service and for having been killed with Fannin. Strangely enough, they were earlier issued 640 acres for his having died at the Alamo. Some early lists of Alamo casualties incorrectly included his name.

His wife, Ann, was killed in a catastrophic accident on a railroad bridge in Norwalk, Connecticut, in 1853, leaving their daughter, Mary, and son-in-law, Samuel R. Keemle, as DeSauque's only heirs.

DESPALLIER, CHARLES (1812–3/6/1836)
Age: 24 years
Born: Louisiana
Residence: Rapides Parish, Louisiana
Rank: Private (rifleman/raider/courier)
KIB

Charles Despallier was the son of Caudida Despallier.

His older brother, Blaz Phillipe Despallier, took part in the siege of Bexar. Charles traveled to Texas to join the army after his brother returned to Louisiana. He reached Bexar in mid-February of 1836.

In his letter to Sam Houston of 2/25/1836, Travis cited Charles Despallier for bravery, stating that he "gallantly sallied out and set fire to houses which afforded the enemy shelter, in the face of enemy fire."[50]

Despallier left the Alamo sometime after 2/25/1836 as a courier, but returned with the relief force from Gonzales on 3/1/1836.

In 1852, headright, bounty, and donation lands were patented to his nephew, Blaz Phillipe Despallier, after the death of Charles's mother.

DEWALL, LEWIS (1812–3/6/1836)
Age: 24 years (plasterer, mason, boatman, blacksmith)
Born: Manhattan, New York
Residence: Vehlein's Colony, Texas
Rank: Private (rifleman, Captain White's infantry company)
KIB

Lewis Dewall was the son of John Dewall, a New York City mason. In 1832 Lewis lived at 51 Lewis Street in Manhattan and worked as a boatman.

He left New York City and traveled to Texas at a time when abolitionist riots and cholera epidemics were sweeping the city. He registered for one league of land in Vehlein's Colony on Harmon's Creek on 10/26/1835, his name being listed as "Duel."

Dewall took part in the siege and battle of Bexar and remained in Bexar as a member of the Bexar Guards.

On various lists and Texas records his name is given as "Duel" or "Dewell," and his occupation in Texas is listed as either a mason or blacksmith.

DICKERSON, ALMERON (1810–3/6/1836)
Age: 26 years (blacksmith)
Born: Tennessee
Residence: Gonzales, Texas
Rank: Captain (artillery officer)
KIB

Almeron Dickerson of Hardeman County, Tennessee, was a blacksmith and a member of the Masons. It is possible that he served in the United States Army as an artilleryman.[51]

On 5/24/1829 he married Susannah A. Wilkerson of Bolivar, Tennessee. He and his wife immigrated to Texas, arriving in DeWitt's Colony on 2/20/1831. On 5/5/1831 they registered for one league of land on the San Marcos River, below the Old Bexar Road.

The Dickersons acquired property in the town of Gonzales on 9/27/1834, where Almeron worked as a blacksmith. He also went into partnership with George C. Kimbell in a hat factory.

On 12/14/1834, Susannah gave birth to a daughter, Angelina Elizabeth.

At the outbreak of the Texas Revolution, Dickerson served as one of the original "Old Eighteen," defenders of the Gonzales cannon. He was in charge of the gun during the actual fight.

In the siege and battle of Bexar, he served as an aid to General Burleson. After the battle, his wife and child joined him in Bexar and lived in the Musquiz house on the southwest corner of Portero Street and the Main Plaza.

At the arrival of Mexican troops on 2/23/1836, Dickerson took his family into the Alamo. He died during the battle of the Alamo, probably while manning the artillery battery in the rear of the Alamo chapel.

Almeron Dickerson's name is often given as "Dickinson" or "Dickenson." At this time there is no verification as to which spelling is correct.

DICKERSON, ANGELINA ELIZABETH (12/14/1834–1871)
Age: 15 months
Born: Gonzales, Texas
Residence: Same
Rank: Civilian (noncombatant, daughter of Capt. Almeron Dickerson)
Survived the Alamo battle

Angelina E. Dickerson was the daughter of Almeron and Susannah Dickerson, and is popularly known as "The Babe of the Alamo."

Before the battle of the Alamo, William B. Travis removed his ring, ran a string through it, and placed the string around her neck. The ring is now on display in the Alamo.

During the battle, she and her mother, along with most of the other women and children, were sheltered in the Alamo chapel.

When her mother was brought before Santa Anna, it is alleged that Santa Anna offered to send Angelina to Mexico to raise as his own.

In 1851, Angelina married John Maynard Griffith and had three children, between 1853 and 1857. She and her husband later divorced. It has been reported that during the Civil War she became a camp follower of Confederate troops.[52] In 1864 she married Oscar Holmes in New Orleans.

Later in life she was praised for her aid of victims of a plague which struck the city of Galveston.

Angelina died at age thirty-seven of a uterine hemorrhage.

DICKERSON, SUSANNAH ARABELLA (1814 or 1815–10/7/1883)

Age: 22 years
Born: Tennessee
Residence: Gonzales, Texas
Rank: Civilian (noncombatant, wife of Capt. Almeron Dickerson)
Survived the Alamo battle (wounded)

Susannah A. Dickerson was the daughter of the Wilkersons of Bolivar, Tennessee. She married Almeron Dickerson on 5/24/1829, and moved to Texas with him. She had one daughter, Angelina Elizabeth, born on 12/14/1834.

The most probable reason for her having accompanied her husband to Bexar and the Alamo was the fact that their home in Gonzales was broken into by a group of men on 11/2/1835, while Captain Dickerson was with the Texan army at the siege of Bexar. Susannah was protected by future Alamo courier Launcelot Smither, who was severely beaten by the men.

When the Mexican army returned to Bexar on 2/23/1836, she and Angelina were taken on horseback to the Alamo by her husband.

Susannah was present during the entire siege and battle of the Alamo, but kept mostly to the chapel. During the battle, her husband rushed to her and stated, "Great God, Sue, the Mexicans are inside our walls! All is lost! If they spare you, save my child."[53]

She witnessed the death of Jacob Walker, who had rushed into her room in the chapel, seeking shelter. He was shot and then bayonetted in front of her. Susannah was wounded by a gunshot to the right calf while being escorted from the Alamo chapel by a Mexican officer.

She was interviewed by Santa Anna after the battle. He gave her two dollars and a blanket, as he did all the noncombatant survivors, and sent her on her way, accompanied by Joe, the slave of Travis. They were met by a scouting party under "Deaf" Smith and were brought to Sam Houston, to whom Susannah gave word of the Alamo defeat.

On 11/27/1837 Susannah married John Williams but divorced on 3/24/1838 due to brutal treatment of herself and her daughter.

On 12/20/1838 she married Francis P. Herring but was widowed again on 9/27/1843.

On 12/15/1847 she married Peter Bellows but was divorced in 1857 by Bellows, who successfully charged her in court with abandonment, adultery, and residing in a "house of ill fame" in Houston.[54]

In 1857 Susannah set up a boardinghouse in Lockhart, Texas, and married Joseph W. Hanning. During the 1870s they moved to Austin and prospered in real estate and other businesses.

On 4/27/1881, Susannah revisted the Alamo with some friends, relatives, and a newspaper reporter to whom she gave an interview describing her experiences at the Alamo.[55]

She died in Austin at age sixty-eight and is buried in Oakwood Cemetery, Austin.

DILLARD, JOHN HENRY (1805–3/6/1836)
Age: 31 years
Born: Smith County, Tennessee
Residence: Nashville-on-the-Brazos, Texas
Rank: Private (rifleman)
KIB

John H. Dillard was the son of William and Sarah Dillard of Tennessee.

DIMITT, PHILIP (1801–7/8/1841)
Age: 35 years (merchant)
Born: Kentucky
Residence: Dimitt's Landing, LaVaca Bay, Texas
Rank: Captain (courier)
Left Alamo on 2/23/1836

Philip Dimitt was an early settler of Texas, arriving in 1822. In 1828 he married Maria Louisa Lazo and they had four children.

Dimitt was a merchant and trader in the LaVaca Bay area, where he set up a trading post called Dimitt's Landing. In the period before the Texas Revolution, he also served as the supplier and contractor for the Mexican garrison at Bexar.

At the outbreak of the revolution, Dimitt was part of the volunteer force which ousted the Mexican force from the town of Goliad. Command of the post eventually fell to him upon the dissolution of the volunteer battalion of the ranking officers assigned.

Philip Dimitt was a strong supporter of Stephen F. Austin. He favored a coalition with the northwestern states of Mexico if Texas was not annexed by the United States, and supported the taking of General Cos at Bexar to panic the central government and stimulate the Mexican liberals. He also favored the Matamoros Expedition.

While in command at Goliad, Dimitt designed a flag of the Mexican tri-color, with the standard, "Constitution of 1824," referring to the liberal constitution of that year which guaranteed Texans their rights. Although unverified, tradition has it that this type of flag flew over the Alamo. If this was the case, it may very well be that Dimitt's banner had that distinction.

Dimitt's heavy-handed command of Goliad brought him into conflict with prominent Mexican citizens and caused Austin to order him to turn over command of the post to Captain Collinsworth in November 1835.[56]

He took part in the siege and battle of Bexar, but returned to Goliad afterward where he, along with other volunteers, signed the controversial "Goliad Declaration," a premature declaration of Texan independence.[57]

On the morning of 1/14/1836, while returning to Goliad, Philip Dimitt met up with Sam Houston, who was en route to the town. Houston ordered Dimitt to raise a company of at least one hundred men and march to Bexar immediately. If the town was invested by the Mexican army, Dimitt was to stay; if not, he was to return to Houston's headquarters.[58]

Dimitt arrived at Bexar with considerably less than the hundred men. Upon the arrival of the Mexican army on 2/23/1836, he was asked by Travis to reconnoiter the enemy. He rode out with Lieutenant Nobles, and they met Dr. Sutherland and David Crockett returning to the Alamo to report to Travis. Dimitt asked the doctor where he was going and told him that there were not enough men to defend the fort. He also stated that he intended to leave and bring reinforcements back to the Alamo.[59]

Dimitt returned to Dimitt's Landing, arriving on 2/28/1836. He commanded a small company for the remainder of the revolution.

On 3/12/1836, he was ordered, with his command, to join Houston at army headquarters. Houston also, unofficially, confided in him that he believed the Alamo had fallen.[60]

On 7/4/1841, while building a new trading post on Corpus Christi Bay, Philip Dimitt and his workers were taken as prisoners by a Mexican raiding party and transported to Saltillo, Mexico. His men escaped after drugging their guards with morphine-laced mescal, but Dimitt remained behind, since he had been confined separately.

Philip Dimitt died in the Mexican prison when he took an overdose of morphine rather than wait to be executed, as the Mexican commander threatened if the escaped men did not return.

DIMPKINS, JAMES R. (?–3/6/1836)
Born: England
Residence: Same

Rank: Sergeant (company NCO, Captain Blazeby's infantry
  company)
KIB

James R. Dimpkins came to Texas by way of New Orleans as a member of Breece's New Orleans Greys.

He took part in the siege and battle of Bexar and remained in Bexar as a sergeant in Blazeby's company.

His name is sometimes listed as "Dimkins," "Dickens," "Dinkin," or "Dockon."

DUVALT, ANDREW (1804–3/6/1836)
Age: 32 years (plasterer)
Born: Ireland
Residence: Gonzales, Texas
Rank: Private (rifleman, Captain White's infantry company)
KIB

Andrew Duvalt came to Texas from Missouri.

He took part in the siege and battle of Bexar and was issued a donation certificate for 640 acres of land for his service. He remained in Bexar as an infantryman in the Bexar Guards.

Sometime after 2/2/1836, he returned home to Gonzales. On 2/23/1836 he was mustered into the Gonzales Ranging Company. He returned to the Alamo, but it is uncertain if he returned as a member of the Gonzales relief force.

His name is sometimes listed as "Devault."

ESPALIER, CARLOS (1819-3/6/1836)
Age: 17 years
Born: San Antonio de Bexar, Texas
Residence: Same
Rank: Private (rifleman)
KIB

Carlos Espalier was said to be a protegé of James Bowie.

His aunt, Doña Guardia de Luz, was his heir. She was granted lands for Espalier's service.

Allegations have been made in the past that Carlos Espalier and Alamo defender Charles Despallier were one and the same. This seems to have arisen merely due to the similarities in their names. No conclusive evidence has ever been put forth to indicate that they were not two distinct people.

ESPARZA, ANA SALAZAR (?–12/12/1847)
Born: San Antonio de Bexar, Texas
Residence: Same
Rank: Civilian (noncombatant, wife of Pvt. Gregorio Esparza)
Survived the Alamo battle

Ana Esparza was the wife of defender Gregorio Esparza. She and her four children entered the Alamo with her husband after twilight on the first day of the siege. Although she was given the opportunity to leave, she chose to stay by her husband's side.

After the Alamo battle, she and her children were brought to the Musquiz house in Bexar, under guard, along with the other women and children from the Alamo.

Ana, responding to the hunger of her children, began to search the Musquiz house for food in defiance of the guards. Finally, Señor Musquiz provided food for all the women and children.

Ana and her children remained in the house until after 3:00 P.M. on 3/6/1836, when she was brought before Santa Anna, questioned, and released. Like the other noncombatants, she was given two silver dollars and a blanket.

After being released, she returned to her home and wept for many days.

Ana died on 12/12/1847.

ESPARZA, ENRIQUE (September 1828–12/20/1917)
Age: 8 years
Born: San Antonio de Bexar, Texas
Residence: Same
Rank: Civilian (noncombatant, son of Pvt. Gregorio Esparza)
Survived the Alamo battle

Enrique Esparza was the oldest son of Gregorio and Ana Salazar Esparza. He entered the Alamo with his parents, brothers, and sister. Earlier, on 2/23/1836, he had witnessed Santa Anna's arrival in Bexar.

During the Alamo battle, he and his family were sheltered in the Alamo chapel. Esparza witnessed the death of an American boy who was by his side. According to Esparza, the boy did not appear much older than he, and all he did was draw a blanket around his shoulders when the Mexican troops burst into the chapel.[61]

As a young man, Enrique Esparza owned property on Nogalitos Street in San Antonio and he made a living as a truck gardener. He married Gertrudis Hernandez (9/10/1820–2/4/1890) and they had five children.

Sometime between 1850 and 1860, Enrique, along with his brothers, Manuel and Francisco, and their families, moved to Atascosa County, Texas, where they farmed and ranched near Pleasanton.

The brothers built a small chapel near their homes for family worship. In 1869 Enrique and his wife donated five acres to the Catholic church, and the Esparzas built a larger church building, called San Augustine, along with a school. His children attended the school, and he was able to teach himself to read and write from their textbooks. He became fluent in Spanish and English.

Esparza's wife died in 1890. In 1897 he moved back to San Antonio, and three years later to Losoya to live with his son, Victor.

In 1905 and 1907, Esparza gave detailed interviews concerning his experiences at the Alamo to the *San Antonio Daily Express*.[64]

He died on 12/20/1917 at age eighty-nine in Losoya, Texas, surrounded by his surviving children.

ESPARZA, FRANCISCO (?–July 1887)
Age: younger than 5 years
Born: San Antonio de Bexar, Texas
Residence: Same
Rank: Civilian (noncombatant, son of Pvt. Gregorio Esparza)
Survived the Alamo battle

Francisco Esparza was the youngest son of Gregorio and

Ana Salazar Esparza. He was present in the Alamo with the rest of his family during the entire siege and battle.

As an adult, Francisco married Petra Zamora (1827–1924) and they had five children. He moved to Atascosa County with his brothers and their families in the 1850s.

At the outbreak of the Civil War, Francisco gave up farming and joined the Confederate army.

After the war, he left his family and settled in Tucson, Arizona. He remarried and reared two children by his second wife.

Francisco Esparza died in July 1887.

ESPARZA, JOSÉ GREGORIO (3/8/1808–3/6/1836)
Age: 27 years
Born: San Antonio de Bexar, Texas
Rank: Private (artilleryman, Captain Seguin's cavalry
  company)
KIB

José Gregorio Esparza was the son of Juan Antonio and Maria Petra Olivas Esparza, and he was known as Gregorio.

He was one of the company of native Texans under the command of Juan Seguin and took part in the siege and battle of Bexar.

In February 1836, when the Mexican army was approaching Bexar, a friend of Gregorio's, William Smith, offered to send a wagon to remove the Esparza family to Nacogdoches. Santa Anna's army arrived first and Smith advised Gregorio that all friends of the Americans should go into the Alamo.

Gregorio followed Smith's advice and entered the Alamo with his family after sunset on 2/23/1836.

According to Enrique Esparza, sometime after 3/3/1836, James Bowie announced that those who wished to leave the Alamo could do so. When asked if he wished to leave, Gregorio Esparza replied, "No, I will stay and die fighting."[63]

Although a member of Seguin's company, Gregorio helped man a cannon in the Alamo chapel during the battle, close to where his wife and children were sheltered.[64]

45

Gregorio's brother Francisco also lived in Bexar and was a member of General Cos's Leal Presidios. When the Mexican army arrived in Bexar, Francisco Esparza and other native Texans in the town were ordered by Santa Anna to hold themselves in readiness in case they were needed.

Despite popular belief, Francisco Esparza did not take part in the assault on the Alamo. In 1858 he took an oath to the fact that he did not willingly join the Mexican forces.

After the battle, Francisco obtained permission from General Cos to look for the body of his brother.

Gregorio Esparza was found in a small room of the Alamo chapel with a bullet wound in his chest and a sword wound to the side.

Francisco, along with other relatives, buried Gregorio in Campo Santo, on the west side of the San Pedro Creek, where Milam Square is now located. He was the only Texan casualty to be buried. All the rest were put into pyres and burned.

In 1857 donation certificates for Gregorio's service and death were rejected. In 1860 this decision was overturned and his heirs received the land grants entitled to them.

ESPARZA, MANUEL (10/19/1830–1886)
Age: 5 years
Born: San Antonio de Bexar, Texas
Residence: Same
Rank: Civilian (noncombatant, son of Pvt. Gregorio
    Esparza)
Survived the Alamo battle

Manuel Esparza was the son of Gregorio and Ana Salazar Esparza.

He entered the Alamo, along with the rest of his family, in the evening of 2/23/1836, and was present during the entire siege and battle of the Alamo.

On 9/7/1853 Esparza married Melchora Leal (1/4/1834– 2/13/1922) and they had eleven children.

During the 1850s he went with his brothers and their families to Atascosa County, where he farmed and ranched. He also built, with his brothers, the church of San Augustine.

Manuel Esparza is described by his descendants as being much like his brother, Enrique. They both liked history and they were both lifelong Democrats.

He died in 1886.

ESPARZA, MARIA de JESUS (CASTRO) (1/11/1826–1849)
Age: 10 years
Born: San Antonio de Bexar, Texas
Residence: Same
Rank: Civilian (noncombatant, daughter of Ana Salazar Esparza)
Survived the Alamo battle

Much confusion surrounds Maria de Jesus Esparza.

Enrique Esparza, in his 1907 interview, claimed that his sister was an infant at the time of the Alamo battle. However, there is no evidence in San Antonio records to indicate that a daughter was ever born to Gregorio and Ana Esparza. Ana Esparza was married once before to Victor de Castro, who died in 1825, and they were the parents of Maria de Jesus Castro. Further, the 1830 Mexican Census of San Antonio indicates that four-year-old Maria de Jesus Castro was part of the household of Gregorio Esparza.[65]

Maria de Jesus Castro, sometimes called Esparza, died in San Antonio in 1849.

EVANS, ROBERT (1800–3/6/1836)
Age: 36 years
Born: Ireland
Residence: New York
Rank: Major (master of ordnance, Ordnance Dept.)
KIB

Robert Evans immigrated to Texas from New York by way of New Orleans. He served as ordnance chief under Lieutenant Colonel Neill after the battle of Bexar and retained tnat position after the command went to Travis.

As ordnance chief, Evans would have been responsible for the maintenance and care of all the cannon, firearms, and munitions within the Alamo.

Susannah Dickerson stated that when the Mexican soldiers broke into the Alamo chapel, Evans attempted to blow up the remaining supply of gunpowder with a torch. He was shot down before he could do so.

Susannah Dickerson described Robert Evans as being black-haired, blue-eyed, nearly six feet tall, and always merry.[66]

EVANS, SAMUEL B. (1/16/1812–3/6/1836)
Age: 24 years
Born: Jefferson County, New York
Residence: Kentucky
Rank: Private (rifleman)
KIB

Samuel B. Evans was the son of Musgrove and Ali Brown Evans. His grandfather, Samuel Evans, was a general in the Colonial army during the Revolutionary War. His uncle, Gen. Jacob Brown, formerly commanded the United States Army.

Samuel's father was the administrator of his estate.

EWING, JAMES L. (1812–3/6/1836)
Age: 24 years
Residence: Tennessee
Rank: Private (artilleryman/secretary to the commanding officer, Captain Carey's artillery company)
KIB

James L. Ewing took part in the siege and battle of Bexar and received a donation certificate for 640 acres of land for his service.

He remained in Bexar as a member of Carey's company, and served as secretary to Lieutenant Colonel Neill. It is possible that he served Travis in that capacity when the command was turned over to him.

FISHBAUGH, WILLIAM (?–3/6/1836)
Residence: Gonzales, Texas
Rank: Private (rifleman, Gonzales Ranging Company)
KIB

William Fishbaugh enlisted in the Gonzales Ranging Company on 2/23/1836. He entered the Alamo with this unit on 3/1/1836.

His name is sometimes listed as "Fishback."

FLANDERS, JOHN (1800–3/6/1836)
Age: 36 years
Born: Salisbury, Massachusetts
Residence: Gonzales, Texas
Rank: Private (rifleman, Gonzales Ranging Company)
KIB

John Flanders was the son of Levi and Mary Sargent Flanders. He was a single man.

Flanders was in business with his father in Massachusetts. He left home after a disagreement with his father in which he wanted to foreclose on a mortgage held on the property of a widow, while his father did not.

John Flanders never communicated with his family again, but he was heard of by them while he was in New Orleans and later in Texas.

He was part of the relief force from Gonzales and entered the Alamo with this unit on 3/1/1836.

FLOYD, DOLPHIN WARD (3/6/1804–3/6/1836)
Age: 32 years (farmer)
Born: Nash County, North Carolina
Residence: Gonzales, Texas
Rank: Private (rifleman, Gonzales Ranging Company)
KIB

Dolphin W. Floyd was the son of Thomas Penuel and Mary Beckwith Floyd. He married Ester Berry House (3/25/1808–1/21/1870) in Gonzales, Texas, on 4/26/1832.

He joined the Gonzales relief force and entered the Alamo with them on 3/1/1836.

Dolphin died at the Alamo on his thirty-second birthday.

His name is sometimes listed as "Dolphin Ward."

Floyd County, Texas, is named in his honor.

FONTLEROY, WILLIAM H. (1814–3/6/1836)

Age: 22 years
Born: Logan County, Kentucky
Residence: Kentucky
Rank: Private (rifleman, Captain Harrison's company, VAC)
KIB

William H. Fontleroy traveled to Texas with Peter J. Bailey, Daniel Cloud, Joseph G. Washington, and B. Archer M. Thomas.

He took the oath of allegiance and was mustered into the Volunteer Auxiliary Corps of Texas at Nacogdoches on 1/14/1836.

He traveled to the Alamo as a member of Captain Harrison's company.

His name is often listed as "Furtleroy" or "Fauntleroy."

FORSYTH, JOHN HUBBARD (8/10/1797–3/6/1836)

Age: 38 years (farmer, nonpracticing doctor)
Born: Avon, Livingston County, New York
Residence: Kentucky
Rank: Captain (commanding officer of cavalry company)
KIB

John H. Forsyth was the oldest child of Alexander and Mary Treat Forsyth. He was reared on his father's farm in Avon, New York. He studied medicine but never practiced.

On 4/3/1822 he married Deborah Smith.

Forsyth left New York in late December 1828 after the death of his wife, leaving his son, Edmond Augustus, with his father's family.

He traveled to Texas from Kentucky as the captain of a company of volunteers in 1835. In Texas he obtained a commission as a regular captain[67] in the Texan cavalry.

Forsyth traveled to the Alamo with his men, accompanying Lieutenant Colonel Travis to the post.

On his way to the Alamo, Forsyth used all of his available cash to outfit and supply his company pending reimbursement from the government of Texas.

FUENTES, ANTONIO (1813–3/6/1836)

Age: 23 years
Born: San Antonio de Bexar, Texas
Residence: Same
Rank: Private (rifleman, Captain Seguin's cavalry company)
KIB

Antonio Fuentes was one of the native Texans recruited by Juan Seguin for six months of service.

He took part in the siege and battle of Bexar as a member of Seguin's company.

Fuentes figured into the rift between Travis and Bowie before the siege of the Alamo began. He had been found guilty of theft by a jury which included both Travis and Bowie and had been sentenced to jail by Seguin, who was acting as judge.

After Bowie was elected commander of the volunteers at Bexar and became excessively drunk, he freed Fuentes from the jail.

Antonio Fuentes was subsequently ordered back to jail by Seguin, but he entered the Alamo with the rest of Seguin's company on 2/23/1836.

FUQUA, GALBA (3/9/1819–3/6/1836)

Age: 16 years
Born: Alabama
Residence: Gonzales, Texas
Rank: Private (rifleman, Gonzales Ranging Company)
KIB

Galba Fuqua was the son of Silas and Sally Taney Fuqua.

He enlisted in the Gonzales Ranging Company on 2/23/1836. He traveled to and entered the Alamo with this unit on 3/1/1836.

During the Alamo battle, according to Susannah Dickerson, Fuqua burst into her room in the chapel and tried to tell her something. She could not understand him since his jaw had been broken. He rushed back to the battle without having conveyed his message.

Galba Fuqua is often misidentified as being of Mexican descent. Evidence points to the fact that he may have actually descended from French Huguenots.[68]

He was one of the youngest defenders of the Alamo, having died days short of his seventeenth birthday.

GARNETT, WILLIAM (1812–3/6/1836)
Age: 24 years (Baptist preacher)
Born: Virginia
Residence: Falls-on-the-Brazos, Robertson's Colony, Texas
Rank: Private (rifleman)
KIB

William Garnett may have been one of the men of Captain Forsyth's company who traveled to the Alamo with Travis.

Once at Bexar, he received a furlough, signed by Travis, and traveled to Velasco. There, he made Massillon Farley his agent, gave him his papers, and assured him that he would return in three months.[69] He returned to Bexar in time for the siege and battle of the Alamo.

William Garnett has been described as a man of unblemished character and a great admirer of Travis.[70]

GARRAND, JAMES W. (1813–3/6/1836)
Age: 23 years
Residence: Louisiana
Rank: Private (rifleman, Captain Blazeby's infantry
    company)
KIB

James W. Garrand took part in the siege and battle of Bexar. He remained in Bexar as a member of Blazeby's company.

GARRETT, JAMES GIRARD (1806–3/6/1836)
Age: 30 years
Born: Tennessee
Residence: Louisiana
Rank: Private (rifleman, Captain Blazeby's infantry
    company)
KIB

James G. Garrett came to Texas as a member of Breece's New Orleans Greys. He took part in the siege and battle of Bexar and remained in Bexar as a member of Blazeby's company.

GARVIN, JOHN E. (1809–3/6/1836)
Age: 27 years
Residence: Gonzales, Texas
Rank: Private (artilleryman, Captain Carey's artillery company)
KIB

John E. Garvin enlisted in the artillery under Lieutenant Colonel Neill in Bexar on 12/14/1835.

He left Bexar for his home in Gonzales but returned to the Alamo on 3/1/1836 as part of the relief force from Gonzales.

GASTON, JOHN E. (1819–3/6/1836)
Age: 17 years
Residence: Gonzales, Texas
Rank: Private (rifleman, Gonzales Ranging Company)
KIB

John E. Gaston was the son of widow Rebecca Warfield Gaston. His stepfather was George Washington Davis.

He was part of the Gonzales relief force and entered the Alamo with this group on 3/1/1836.

GEORGE, JAMES (1802–3/6/1836)
Age: 34 years
Residence: Gonzales, Texas
Rank: Private (rifleman, Gonzales Ranging Company)
KIB

James George was the son of William and Elizabeth Bland George. On 2/29/1821 he married Elizabeth Dearduff, sister of Alamo defender William Dearduff.

During the actions in the fall of 1835, a yoke of oxen and

a set of gearing owned by George was pressed into service in order to haul the Gonzales cannon.

George was part of the relief force from Gonzales and entered the Alamo with this group on 3/1/1836.

GONZALES, PETRA
Age: Elderly
Residence: San Antonio de Bexar, Texas
Rank: Civilian (noncombatant)
Survived the Alamo battle

Not much is known about Petra Gonzales. Enrique Esparza remembered her as being in the Alamo and that she was an old woman. He only remembered her as being called Doña Petra. There is a possibility that she may have been an elderly relative of Ana S. Esparza.[71]

GOODRICH, JOHN C. (1809–3/6/1836)
Age: 27 years
Born: Virginia
Residence: Anderson, Grimes County, Texas
Rank: Cornett[72] (company officer/guidon bearer, possibly
   Captain Forsyth's cavalry company)
KIB

John C. Goodrich was the son of John Goodrich. Before coming to Texas he lived in Tennessee.

In 1826 he was recommended as a purser in the United States Navy by then Tennessee Congressman Sam Houston. Goodrich, however, did not serve in the navy. He moved to Texas with his brother, Benjamin Briggs Goodrich, settling in Grimes County on 4/30/1834.

In Texas he apparently kept up his acquaintance with Houston. On 11/28/1835, in a letter to Houston, John Goodrich offered his service to the army, "in any other attitude than a common soldier."[73]

He received a commission in the rank of cornett in the Texan regular army.

He may have entered Bexar and the Alamo in early February 1836 as a member of Captain Forsyth's company. There is some evidence that he might have been part of Captain Blazeby's infantry company and already in Bexar.[74]

While Goodrich was besieged in the Alamo, his brother was one of the signers of the Texas Declaration of Independence on 3/2/1836.

GRIMES, ALBERT CALVIN (12/20/1817–3/6/1836)
Age: 18 years
Born: Georgia
Residence: Texas (near present Navasota)
Rank: Private (rifleman, possibly Captain Forsyth's cavalry company)
KIB

Albert C. Grimes was the son of Jesse and Martha Smith Grimes.

He may have come to Bexar and the Alamo as a member of Forsyth's company.

While Albert was besieged in the Alamo, his father was one of the signers of the Texas Declaration of Independence on 3/2/1836.

GUERRERO, BRIGIDO
Former Mexican soldier
Born: Tallenango, Mexico
Residence: San Antonio de Bexar, Texas
Rank: Private (rifleman)
Survived Alamo battle

Brigido Guerrero either came to Texas in 1832 with the Mexican forces under Domingo Ugartechea, to build Fort Velasco, or in 1835 with Mexican reinforcements under Ugartechea.

At the outbreak of the Texas Revolution he apparently deserted the Mexican army and joined the Texan revolutionaries.

In early 1836 he was with James Bowie and was employed in obtaining cattle for the Bexar garrison.

During the final stages of the Alamo battle, Guerrero took refuge in the Alamo chapel. He managed to convince the Mexican soldiers that he was a prisoner of the Texans, and they spared his life.

In 1846 Guerrero married Dolores Mendez y Montoya. In 1851 they had a daughter, Maria Faustina, and over the next ten years they had several other children.

The Guerreros lived in a house near the Alamo *acequia*[75] until 1853, when they sold it and moved to another site nearby. They were still living at their new location in 1870.

In 1861 Brigido Guerrero stated that perhaps one other man, an American, survived the Alamo battle.

In 1874 he testified, along with a witness, as to his participation in the Texas Revolution.[76] One year later he received a pension from the State of Texas based on his participation in the battles of Bexar and Concepcion, but not for the Alamo, since only families of those who died at the Alamo were eligible.

Brigido Guerrero is often confused with José Maria Guerrero, who had earlier served in Seguin's cavalry company, but who did not take part in the Alamo battle.

GWYNNE, JAMES C. (1804–3/6/1836)
Age: 32 years
Born: England
Residence: Mississippi
Rank: Private (artilleryman, Captain Carey's artillery
    company)
KIB

James C. Gwynne moved to Texas from Mississippi.

He took part in the siege and battle of Bexar and remained in Bexar as a member of Carey's company.

His name is sometimes listed as "Gwin," "Groya," or "Groyn."

HANNUM, JAMES (8/8/1815–3/6/1836)
Age: 20 years
Born: Pennsylvania

Rank: Private (rifleman)
KIB

James Hannum was the son of Washington Lee and Martha Robertson Hannun.

It is uncertain how he came to Bexar and the Alamo and to which unit he belonged.

His name is sometimes listed as "Hannan" and "Hanuam."

HARRIS, JOHN (1813–3/6/1836)
Age: 23 years
Born: Kentucky
Residence: Gonzales, Texas
Rank: Private (rifleman, Gonzales Ranging Company)
KIB

John Harris took part in the siege and battle of Bexar and was issued a donation certificate for 640 acres of land for his service. He remained in Bexar as a member of the Bexar Guards.

Sometime before the siege of the Alamo began, John returned to his home in Gonzales. On 2/23/1836 he was mustered into the Gonzales Ranging Company. He returned to Bexar and the Alamo with this group on 3/1/1836.

HARRISON, ANDREW JACKSON (1809–3/6/1836)
Age: 27 years
Born: Tennessee
Rank: Private (rifleman)
KIB

It is uncertain how Andrew J. Harrison came to Bexar and the Alamo and to which unit he belonged.

His heirs were issued land bounty donation certificate #519 by the Texas Adjutant General on 9/12/1853, but the commissioner of claims, W. S. Hotchkiss, incorrectly rejected the certificate on 10/26/1860, writing, "no law for giving donation for dying in the service."[77]

His heirs did receive 320 acres for "his service until 6

March 1836 and having fallen at the Alamo."[78] They should have received 320 acres for his service and 640 acres for his death in the service.[79]

HARRISON, WILLIAM B. (1811–3/6/1836)
Age: 25 years
Born: Ohio
Residence: Tennessee
Rank: Captain (company commander, VAC company)
KIB

William B. Harrison was the commanding officer of the company known as the Tennessee Mounted Volunteers. His company was made up of recent arrivals in Texas who were sworn into the service on 1/14/1836 at Nacogdoches.

He and his company rode from Nacogdoches to Washington-on-the-Brazos, leaving there on 1/20/1836 for San Antonio de Bexar. They arrived in Bexar on or about 2/9/1836 and entered the Alamo on 2/23/1836.

During the siege and battle of the Alamo, Harrison's company defended the wooden palisade which ran from the Alamo chapel to the low barracks, the Alamo's south wall.

HAWKINS, JOSEPH M. (1799–3/6/1836)
Age: 37 years
Born: Ireland
Rank: Private (rifleman, possibly Captain Baker's company)
KIB

Joseph M. Hawkins came to Texas by way of Louisiana, and may have been one of the volunteers who accompanied James Bowie to Bexar and the Alamo. He was a staunch supporter of Governor Henry Smith.

On letters and documents he signed his name as "M. Hawkins." There is some evidence that the "M" stood for "Mark."

HAYS, JOHN M. (1814–3/6/1836)
Age: 22 years (possibly a lawyer)
Born: Nashville, Tennessee
Residence: Same
Rank: Private (rifleman, possibly Captain Baker's company)
KIB

John M. Hays was the son of Andrew Hays of Tennessee. He joined Captain Chenoweth's company on 1/14/1836. He may have been one of the volunteers who accompanied James Bowie to Bexar and the Alamo.

On 2/1/1836 he was an unsuccessful candidate for one of the two positions of delegates to the Texas Convention, representing the Bexar garrison.

HEISKELL, CHARLES M. (1813–3/6/1836)
Age: 23 years
Born: possibly Tennessee
Rank: Private (rifleman)
KIB

Charles M. Heiskell was the son of George and Elizabeth Fry Heiskell.

He had been a member of Captain Carey's artillery company, but left Bexar on the ill-fated Matamoros Expedition. He returned to Bexar and the Alamo with the volunteers accompanying James Bowie on 1/19/1836.

His name is also listed as "Haskell" and "Huskill."

HERNDON, PATRICK HENRY (March 1802–3/6/1836)
Age: 34 years
Born: Virginia
Residence: Navidad, Texas
Rank: Private (rifleman, possibly Captain Baker's company)
KIB

Patrick H. Herndon was the son of John and Judith Hampton Herndon. He married Parmelia Smith of Kentucky on 11/1/1824.

Herndon joined the Texas army at Bexar on 12/15/1835 and Captain Chenoweth's company on 1/14/1836.

He may have been one of the volunteers who accompanied James Bowie to Bexar and the Alamo on 1/19/1836.

HERSEE, WILLIAM DANIEL (1805–3/6/1836)
Age: 31 years
Born: England
Residence: New York
Rank: Sergeant (company NCO, Captain Carey's artillery
  company)
KIB

William D. Hersee was a married man with four children. He came to Texas by way of Louisiana.

He took part in the siege and battle of Bexar and was wounded in the battle.

It is not known if Hersee's wounds prevented him from taking an active part in the battle of the Alamo.

HIGHSMITH, BENJAMIN FRANKLIN (9/11/1817–
  11/20/1905)
Age: 18 years
Born: St. Charles District, Missouri Territory
Residence: Bastrop, Texas
Rank: Private (courier)
Left Bexar as a courier, probably just before the siege began

Benjamin F. Highsmith was the son of Ahijah M. and Deborah Turner Highsmith. His father had been a scout and ranger during the War of 1812.

He and his family traveled to Texas by wagon train and crossed the Sabine River by raft on 12/24/1823. They settled on the Colorado River near present-day La Grange.

In 1830 Highsmith first visited Bexar with a group which included James Bowie, William Barret Travis, and George C. Kimble.

At age fifteen, he joined the company of Aylett C. Buckner and took part in the battle of Velasco on 6/26/1832. In 1832 he settled in Bastrop, Texas, and lived there for the next fifty years.

During the Texas Revolution, Highsmith took part in the fight for the Gonzales cannon, the battle of Concepcion, the Grass Fight,[80] and the siege and battle of Bexar. He remained in Bexar after the town was taken by the Texans, but it is unclear if he belonged to any specific unit.

On or about 2/18/1836, Highsmith was sent out by Travis with an appeal for help to Colonel Fannin at Goliad. Upon his return to Bexar, he found the Mexican army already in possession of the town. He was spotted by the Mexican cavalry at Powder House Hill and was pursued by them for about six miles.

He returned to Gonzales and there, on 3/1/1836, met James B. Bonham, who was returning to Bexar.

After the fall of the Alamo, Highsmith served General Houston as a courier. He and David B. Kent, son of Alamo defender Andrew Kent, carried a message from Houston to Fannin ordering Fannin to abandon Goliad, destroy the defenses, and fall back to the Guadalupe River.

He took part in the battle of San Jacinto as a member of Capt. William Ware's company.

After the Texas Revolution, Benjamin Highsmith had a long career with the Texas Rangers.

He served in the Mexican War and took part in the battles of Palo Alto, Monterey, and was wounded at Buena Vista.

In 1853 he married Elizabeth Turner and they had thirteen children. He and his family moved to Bandera County in 1882.

Highsmith died in Uvalde County, Texas, at age eighty-eight.

HOLLAND, TAPLEY (1810–3/6/1836)
Age: 26 years
Born: Ohio
Residence: Grimes County, Texas
Rank: Private (artilleryman, Captain Carey's artillery
  company)
KIB

Tapley Holland was one of six children of Francis and

Frances Buck Holland. His father was born in Canada and came to Texas from Louisiana in 1822 as one of Stephen F. Austin's original 300 settlers.

Tapley Holland took part in the siege and battle of Bexar and remained in Bexar as a member of Carey's company.

HOLLOWAY, SAMUEL (1808–3/6/1836)

Age: 28 years
Born: Philadelphia, Pennsylvania
Rank: Private (rifleman, Captain Blazeby's infantry
   company)
KIB

Samuel Holloway was the son of James S. and Martha Owen Spencer Holloway. He came to Texas by way of Louisiana as a member of Breece's New Orleans Greys.

He took part in the siege and battle of Bexar and remained in Bexar as a member of Blazeby's company.

HOWELL, WILLIAM D. (1791–3/6/1836)

Age: 45 years (doctor)
Born: Massachusetts
Residence: New York
Rank: Possibly surgeon (rifleman/possibly surgeon, Captain
   Blazeby's infantry company)
KIB

William D. Howell came to Texas by way of New Orleans as a member of Breece's company of New Orleans Greys.

He took part in the siege and battle of Bexar and remained in Bexar as a member of Blazeby's company.

During the siege of the Alamo, he may have served in the capacity of surgeon.

Howell was married and had several children, most of whom had died by the time land claims were filed in his name in 1881. The wife and children of his son, Ananias, became his heirs.

In 1885 Mrs. E. A. Powell (formerly Howell), apparently the surviving daughter of William Howell, filed claim against the heirs of Ananias Howell and received a good portion of the land previously granted to them for Howell's service.

JACKSON, THOMAS (?–3/6/1836)
Born: Ireland
Residence: Gonzales, Texas
Rank: Private (rifleman, Gonzales Ranging Company)
KIB

Thomas Jackson registered in DeWitt's Colony on 5/1/1831.

He married Louise Cottle, sister of Alamo defender George W. Cottle, and was the father of four children.

Jackson was one of the "Old Eighteen" defenders of the Gonzales cannon. He entered the Alamo as a member of the relief force from Gonzales on 3/1/1836.

JACKSON, WILLIAM DANIEL (1807–3/6/1836)
Age: 29 years (former sailor)
Residence: Kentucky
Rank: Private (artilleryman, Captain Carey's artillery company)
KIB

William D. Jackson may have been a native of Ireland, or his place of birth may have been confused with that of Thomas Jackson on early muster rolls.

He took part in the siege and battle of Bexar and remained in Bexar as a member of Carey's company.

JAMESON, GREEN B. (1807–3/6/1836)
Age: 29 years (lawyer)
Born: Kentucky
Residence: Brazoria, Texas
Rank: Major (chief engineer, staff officer)
KIB

Green B. Jameson was the son of Benjamin Jameson of New Jersey. His grandfather, John Jameson, was an early lieutenant governor of Virginia. He came to Texas in 1830 and set up a law practice in San Felipe.

Jameson took part in the siege and battle of Bexar. He remained in Bexar as chief engineer under Neill and, later, Travis. As such, he was in charge of the fortifications at the Alamo.

In a letter to Sam Houston on 1/18/1836, Jameson gave a detailed description of the defenses of the Alamo and the condition of the garrison.[81]

On the first day of the siege of the Alamo, James Bowie utilized him as a messenger to the Mexican troops.

On most muster rolls and lists, Green Jameson is listed as an "ensign," as all engineers of the Texas army were designated.

JENNINGS, GORDON C. (1780–3/6/1836)
Age: 56 years (farmer)
Born: Pennsylvania
Residence: Austin's Colony, Texas
Rank: 1st Corporal (company NCO, Captain Carey's
    artillery company)
KIB

Gordon C. Jennings was the son of Degress Jennings of Virginia. He was married to Catherine Cynthic and they had two sons and two daughters.

Jennings came to Texas from Missouri in 1835.

He took part in the siege and battle of Bexar and remained in Bexar as a member of Carey's company.

Gordon Jennings was the oldest Alamo defender at age fifty-six. His brother, Charles B. Jennings, was one of those executed by the Mexican troops at Goliad.

JOE (1813 or 1815–?)
Age: 21–23 years (slave)
Born: Southern United States
Residence: San Felipe, Texas
Rank: Civilian (rifleman)
Survived the Alamo battle (wounded)

Joe was born into slavery somewhere in the southern United States. He was recorded as a resident of Harrisburg, Texas, in May 1833.

An entry in the diary of William B. Travis for 2/13/1834 states that he "wrote bond for J. W. Moore to sheriff indemnifying him to buy one boy Joe belonging to Mansfield."[82]

Joe accompanied Travis to Bexar and the Alamo in February 1836.

At the beginning of the Alamo battle on the morning of 3/6/1836, Joe, armed with a rifle, went with Travis to their position on the north wall of the fortress. He witnessed Travis's death at this position and then took cover in one of the rooms of the Alamo.

Joe continued to fire his rifle from this position but was isolated from the rest of the battle. He remained there until a Mexican officer entered the room and asked if there were any Negroes there. When Joe stood up, he was slightly wounded by a bayonet and a rifle shot by some of the over-anxious Mexican soldiers. The Mexican officer controlled his troops and took Joe prisoner.

Joe was brought before Santa Anna, questioned, and then made to watch a parade of Mexican troops to impress upon him the strength of the Mexican army. He was released and accompanied Susannah and Angelina Dickerson to the camp of Sam Houston.

Joe took word of the Alamo's fall to Texan officials at Washington-on-the-Brazos and gave a very clear account of his participation to the Texan cabinet at Groce's Retreat.[83]

Joe eventually went to John Rice Jones as part of Travis's estate. He escaped on 4/21/1837 and made his way east, carrying the word of Travis's death to the Travis family in Alabama.

Joe was last reported in Texas, in Austin, in 1875.

He is said to be buried in an unmarked grave near Brewton, Alabama.

Joe was described by John Rice Jones as "five feet ten or eleven inches high, very black and good countenance."[84]

JOHN (?–3/6/1836)
Store clerk, possibly a slave
Residence: Probably Matagorda, Texas
Rank: Civilian (rifleman)
KIB

Most early lists of Alamo defenders list a man named "John," with no last name and an identification that he was a clerk in DeSauque's store.

It was not until the 1930s that this defender began to be listed as a Negro slave.[85] No other information is ever given.

In the early lists of Alamo defenders, many men are listed by last name only. John is the only casualty listed by a first name. There are also many mistakes in these early lists, such as misspellings, listings of some names twice with slight variations in spelling, and even the listing of some men (such as DeSauque) who did not die at the Alamo.[86]

These facts plus a lack of any substantial information on John leave open many possibilities. John may have been: a slave of DeSauque who worked as a clerk in his store; a free black who worked for DeSauque; a slave owned by some other defender and mistakenly thought to have belonged to DeSauque; or a defender who was listed solely by his first name on a list with plenty of mistakes.

There is, however, nothing to preclude the fact that John was not a slave who died in the Alamo in the name of freedom. Joe, Travis's slave, stated that there were other Negroes in the Alamo besides himself.[87]

JOHNSON, LEWIS (1811–3/6/1836)
Age: 25 years
Born: Wales
Residence: Nacogdoches, Texas
Rank: Private (possibly an artilleryman in Captain Carey's artillery company)
KIB

Lewis Johnson enlisted in the service of Texas on 9/28/1835 and served in Captain Coleman's company. He took part in the siege and battle of Bexar and enlisted for an additional four months, possibly as a member of Carey's company.

Johnson was the only native of Wales to die in the Alamo battle.

JOHNSON, WILLIAM (?–3/6/1836)
Born: Philadelphia, Pennsylvania
Rank: Private (possibly an artilleryman in Captain Carey's artillery company)
KIB

William Johnson moved to Texas from Pennsylvania. He may have served as a member of Carey's company.

JOHNSON, WILLIAM P. (?–3/27/1836)
Possibly a sergeant (courier)
Possibly left Alamo as a courier on 2/23/1836

Dr. John Sutherland stated that when he and John W. Smith were sent to Gonzales, a courier named "Johnson" was sent to Fannin at Goliad at the same time.

A muster roll of Capt. Amon B. King's company in Fannin's command lists a sergeant, William P. "Johnston." It is possible that he was sent by Fannin to Bexar with a communication for Travis and then sent back to Fannin when the Mexican army arrived. However, the evidence is too flimsy to make any definite conclusions.

William P. Johnson, whether he was an Alamo courier or not, died in the executions at Goliad.

JONES, JOHN (1810–3/6/1836)
Age: 26 years
Born: New York
Rank: 1st Lieutenant (company officer, Captain Blazeby's infantry company)
KIB

John Jones came to Texas by way of New Orleans as a sergeant in Breece's company of New Orleans Greys. He took part in the siege and battle of Bexar. He remained in Bexar and was promoted to first lieutenant in Blazeby's infantry company.

His name is not mentioned in Texas land bounty records.

There is much confusion as to the records of this defender, since there were at least five "John Joneses" in the Texan army during 1836.

KELLOGG, JOHN BENJAMIN (1817–3/6/1836)
Age: 19 years
Born: Kentucky
Residence: Gonzales, Texas
Rank: Private (rifleman, Gonzales Ranging Company)
KIB

John B. Kellogg was the son of John B. Kellogg, Sr.

In 1835 he married Sidney Gaston (1816–1838), the former wife of Alamo defender Thomas R. Miller.

Kellogg joined the relief force from Gonzales and entered the Alamo with this group on 3/1/1836.

KENNY, JAMES (1814–3/6/1836)
Age: 22 years
Born: Virginia
Residence: Washington-on-the-Brazos, Texas
Rank: Private (rifleman)
KIB

James Kenny was the son of James Kenny, Sr., of Kentucky.

He was a single man and moved to Texas from Virginia in 1834.

He enlisted in the service of Texas on 9/28/1835 and served in Captain Coleman's company until 12/14/1835. He then reenlisted for another four months of service.

A riding whip which belonged to Kenny is on display in the Alamo today.

KENT, ANDREW (Late 1790s–3/6/1836)
Age: 34–38 years (farmer, possibly a carpenter)
Born: Kentucky
Residence: Gonzales, Texas
Rank: Private (rifleman, Gonzales Ranging Company)
KIB

Andrew Kent was the son of Isaac and Lucy Hopkins Kent.

In 1816 he married Elizabeth Zumwalt of Kentucky in Montgomery County, Missouri.

He and his family left their Missouri farm to move to Texas and settle in Gonzales. Kent farmed, but also may have done some work as a carpenter.[88]

On 2/23/1836 he was mustered into the Gonzales Ranging Company along with his son David. He rode to the Alamo with this group, arriving on 3/1/1836.

KERR, JOSEPH (1814–3/6/1836)
Age: 22 years
Born: Lake Providence, Louisiana
Residence: Same
Rank: Private (rifleman)
KIB

Joseph Kerr was the son of General Kerr of Lake Providence, Louisiana. He traveled to Texas with his brother, Nathaniel, as members of the Louisiana Volunteers for Texas Independence, under the command of Capt. S. L. Chamblis.

On or about 2/1/1836, Joseph and his brother were honorably discharged from this group due to the disability of their horses. They were sent by Captain Chamblis to join the troops at Bexar.

On 2/19/1836 Nathaniel died of a sudden illness. Joseph remained as part of the garrison at Bexar and entered the Alamo four days later.

Joseph Kerr's nephew, James D. Kerr, and his niece, Harriett Kerr Davisson, were his heirs.

KIMBELL, GEORGE C. (1803–3/6/1836)
Age: 33 years
Born: Pennsylvania
Residence: Gonzales, Texas
Rank: Lieutenant (commanding officer of ranging company,
  Gonzales Ranging Company)
KIB

George C. Kimbell came to Texas from New York and settled in Gonzales. He owned and operated a hat factory on Water Street in Gonzales in partnership with Almeron Dickerson.

On 6/26/1832 he married Prudence Nash. They had two children.

He was mustered into the Gonzales Ranging Company on 2/23/1836 as a lieutenant and commanding officer.

On 2/27/1836 Kimbell received fifty-two pounds of coffee from Stephen Smith as part of the supplies for the men who volunteered to go to the relief of Bexar. He led the relief force from Gonzales, accompanied by Capt. Albert Martin and John W. Smith, who were returning to the Alamo. They arrived at the Alamo on 3/1/1836.

Kimble County, Texas, was named in his honor.

KING, WILLIAM PHILIP (10/8/1820–3/6/1836)
Age: 15 years
Born: Texas
Residence: Gonzales, Texas
Rank: Private (rifleman, Gonzales Ranging Company)
KIB

William P. King was the son of John Gladden and Parmelia Parchman King.

He lived ten to fifteen miles north of the town of Gonzales.

William took the place of his father when the elder King was about to ride to the Alamo with the relief force from Gonzales, in order for his father to be able to look after the rest of his family.

He entered the Alamo on 3/1/1836, and is recognized as the youngest defender of the Alamo.

LEWIS, WILLIAM IRVINE (6/24/1806–3/6/1836)
Age: 29 years
Born: Virginia
Residence: Philadelphia, Pennsylvania
Rank: Private (rifleman, Volunteers accompanying James Bowie)
KIB

William I. Lewis was the son of Dr. Charles W. and Mary Bullen Irvine Lewis.

He was visiting a friend in North Carolina when he decided to leave for Texas.

The *Telegraph and Texas Register* (10/21/1840) carried a letter from Lewis's mother, begging for a memento of her son. A small monument carved from a stone from the Alamo ruins was sent to her.

LIGHTFOOT, WILLIAM J. (1811–3/6/1836)
Age: 25 years
Born: Virginia
Residence: Gonzales, Texas
Rank: 3rd Corporal (company NCO, Captain Carey's artillery company)
KIB

William J. Lightfoot was the son of Elijah and Rebecca Walker Ligon Lightfoot.

He took part in the siege and battle of Bexar and remained in Bexar as a corporal in Carey's company.

His name is sometimes listed as "John W. Lightfoot."

LINDLEY, JONATHAN L. (February 1814–3/6/1836)
Age: 22 years (surveyor)
Born: Sangamon County, Illinois
Residence: Gonzales, Texas
Rank: Private (artilleryman, Captain Carey's artillery company)
KIB

Jonathan L. Lindley was the eldest of ten children of Samuel Washington and Mary Elizabeth Hall Lindley. His family came to Texas in 1833, settling in Montgomery County.

On 7/13/1835, Lindley, a single man, was granted one-quarter league of land in Polk County, Texas.

He took part in the siege and battle of Bexar and, on 12/14/1835, enlisted in the regular Texas army as a member of Carey's company.

Lindley left Bexar and returned home during the Christmas season of 1835. He returned to the Alamo with the relief force from Gonzales on 3/1/1836.

LINN, WILLIAM (?–3/6/1836)
Residence: Boston, Massachusetts
Rank: Private (rifleman, Captain Blazeby's infantry
   company)
KIB

William Linn came to Texas by way of New Orleans as a member of Breece's company of New Orleans Greys.

He took part in the siege and battle of Bexar and was possibly taken prisoner by the Mexican forces for a time.

After the battle he remained in Bexar as a member of Blazeby's company.

LOCKHART, BYRD (1782–1839)
Age: 54 years (surveyor)
Born: Virginia or Missouri
Residence: Gonzales, Texas
Rank: Captain (courier)
Left Alamo as a courier

Byrd Lockhart came to Texas from Missouri after meeting Green DeWitt in New Orleans. He settled in DeWitt's Colony on 3/20/1826.

A widower, he came to Texas with his mother, sister, and two children.

On 12/12/1826 he was commissioned deputy surveyor

and surveyed the lands around the town of Gonzales. On 1/27/1827 Lockhart was chairman of a meeting denouncing the Fredonian Movement,[89] and pledging support to the Mexican government. In April he was in charge of block houses in Gonzales as protection against Indians. In that same year, he also opened a road from Bexar through Gonzales along the right bank of the LaVaca River to Matagorda Bay. Three years later he received four leagues of land along Plum Creek in payment.

In April 1831 Byrd Lockhart was appointed surveyor to DeWitt's Colony by José Antonio Navarro, and then municipal surveyor of District No. 3 in September.

At the outbreak of the Texas Revolution, his services were requested by Colonel Fannin to act as a "pilot" or scout in the actions below Bexar. At this time Lockhart was serving with Stephen F. Austin but became separated from Austin's command near the Medina River on 11/12/1835.

During the siege and battle of Bexar, Lockhart was a private, along with his son Byrd, Jr., in Captain York's company.

On 1/17/1836 James W. Robinson appointed Lockhart commissioner, along with James C. Neill, John W. Smith, and Francisco Ruiz, to treat with Comanche Indians who were threatening Bexar at the time.

On 2/4/1836 he was named commissioner, along with Mathew Caldwell and William A. Mathews, to raise volunteers in the towns of Gonzales and Milam for the Ranging Corps.

He mustered into service the Gonzales Ranging Company of Mounted Volunteers on 2/23/1836.

Sometime within the next two weeks, Byrd Lockhart returned to Bexar and the Alamo. Although he has never been recorded as doing so, it is possible that he rode to the Alamo with the Gonzales Ranging Company. He and Andrew Sowell were sent from the Alamo a short time before the battle in order to obtain supplies for the garrison. They were delayed in Gonzales, buying cattle and supplies, and were unable to return to the Alamo before its fall.

Later, Lockhart served as the captain of a spy company in the Texan army.

He died in 1839. The town of Lockhart, Texas, is named in his honor.

LOSOYA, TORIBIO (1808–3/6/1836)
Age: 28 years
Born: San Antonio de Bexar, Texas
Residence: Same
Rank: Private (rifleman, Captain Seguin's cavalry company)
KIB

Toribio Losoya was the son of Bentura and Concepcion Charli Losoya.

He, his parents, brother Juan, and sister Maria occupied two rooms inside the southwest corner of the Alamo mission. The battles of 1835 and 1836 forced them from their home.

Losoya was married to Francesca Curbier.

At the outbreak of the Texas Revolution, he was one of the company of native Texans enlisted by Juan Seguin for six months of service.

He took part in the siege and battle of Bexar and entered the Alamo as a member of Seguin's company.

After the battle, his body was found in the Alamo chapel by Francisco Ruiz, the *alcalde* of San Antonio de Bexar.

MAIN, GEORGE WASHINGTON (1807–3/6/1836)
Age: 29 years
Born: Virginia
Rank: Lieutenant (company officer, Captain White's
  infantry company)
KIB

George W. Main took part in the siege and battle of Bexar. He was severely wounded in the battle, and because of his wounds he probably did not play a very active role in the Alamo battle.

His heirs did not settle their bounty and donation land claims until 11/26/1875 and 5/8/1893.

MALONE, WILLIAM T. (8/13/1817–3/6/1836)
Age: 18 years
Born: Athens, Georgia
Residence: Alabama
Rank: Private (artilleryman, Captain Carey's artillery
  company)
KIB

William T. Malone was the son of Thomas Hill and Elizabeth Tucker Malone of Virginia. He left his family home in Alabama for New Orleans after becoming drunk and fearing to face his father. His father followed him to New Orleans, but William had already left for Texas by the fall of 1835.

Malone corresponded only once to his family while in Texas, and his mother, according to family tradition, carried this letter on her person until it was worn out.

William Malone took part in the siege and battle of Bexar as a member of Captain Parrott's artillery company. He received a donation certificate for 640 acres of land for his service. He remained in Bexar as a member of Carey's company.

Malone is described as having dark hair and complexion and was said to be wild and wayward.

He was identified as having been in Bexar and the Alamo by Benjamin Highsmith, who recalled that Malone was missing the little finger of his left hand.[90]

MARSHALL, WILLIAM (1808–3/6/1836)
Age: 28 years
Born: Tennessee
Residence: Arkansas
Rank: Private (rifleman, Captain Blazeby's infantry
  company)
KIB

William Marshall came to Texas by way of New Orleans as a member of Breece's New Orleans Greys.

He took part in the siege and battle of Bexar and remained in Bexar as a member of Blazeby's company.

No bounty or donation land was ever recorded for this defender.

MARTIN, ALBERT (1/6/1808–3/6/1836)
Age: 28 years (general store owner)
Born: Providence, Rhode Island
Residence: Gonzales, Texas
Rank: Captain (courier)
KIB

Albert Martin was the son of Joseph S. and Abbey B. Martin.

He arrived in Texas in early 1835 by way of Tennessee and New Orleans, following his father and older brothers. He settled in Gonzales in May 1835.

Martin was one of the leaders of the "Old Eighteen," original defenders of the Gonzales cannon, in September 1835. He was part of the Texan army at the siege of Bexar, but was back in Gonzales by 12/19/1835, recovering from an injury to his foot by an ax. He returned to Bexar sometime before the Alamo siege began.

On 2/23/1836 he was utilized as an emissary by Travis to the Mexican force. He met Col. Juan N. Almonte of the Mexican army, who rejected Martin's suggestion that he accompany Martin to the Alamo and speak dierctly with Travis.

On 2/24/1836 Martin carried the famous message of Travis to Gonzales and there passed it on to Launcelot Smither.[91]

Martin returned to the Alamo as senior officer, accompanying the relief force from Gonzales.

McCAFFERTY, EDWARD (?–3/6/1836)
Residence: Refugio County, Texas
Rank: Lieutenant
KIB

Edward McCafferty may have been an officer of the volunteers who accompanied James Bowie to the Alamo.

No bounty or donation land was ever recorded for this defender.

McCOY, JESSE (1804–3/6/1836)
Age: 32 years (town sheriff)
Born: Gyrosburg, Tennessee
Residence: Gonzales, Texas
Rank: Private (rifleman, Gonzales Ranging Company)
KIB

Jesse McCoy was the son of John and Martha McCoy.
He was an original settler of DeWitt's Colony, Texas, arriving there on 3/9/1827 from Missouri.
On 2/23/1836 he was mustered in as a member of the Gonzales Ranging Compnay. He entered the Alamo with this unit on 3/1/1836.

McDOWELL, WILLIAM (1794–3/6/1836)
Age: 43 years
Born: Mifflin County, Pennsylvania
Residence: Tennessee
Rank: Private (rifleman, Captain Harrison's company, VAC)
KIB

William McDowell was the son of Col. John McDowell of Kishacoguillas Valley, Pennsylvania. He left Tennessee for Texas with John P. Reynolds in 1835.
On 1/14/1836 he was sworn into the Volunteer Auxiliary Corps of Texas at Nacogdoches before Judge Forbes.
He rode to Bexar and the Alamo as a member of Captain Harrison's company, arriving there on or about 2/9/1836.

McGEE, JAMES (?–3/6/1836)
Born: Ireland
Rank: Private (rifleman, Captain Blazeby's infantry company)
KIB

James McGee came to Texas by way of New Orleans as a member of Breece's New Orleans Greys.
He took part in the siege and battle of Bexar and remained in Bexar as a member of Blazeby's company. He was

wounded in the battle of Bexar, and it is not known if he was an active participant in the Alamo siege and battle.

McGREGOR, JOHN (1808–3/6/1836)
Age: 28 years
Born: Scotland
Residence: Nacogdoches, Texas
Rank: 2nd Sergeant (company NCO, Captain Carey's artillery company)
KIB

John McGregor took part in the siege and battle of Bexar. He was issued a donation certificate for 640 acres of land for his part in the battle. He remained in Bexar as a sergeant in Carey's company.

An enduring story of the Alamo describes McGregor as playing his bagpipes while accompanied by David Crockett on the fiddle, to lift the spirits of the men during the siege.

McKINNEY, ROBERT (1809–3/6/1836)
Age: 27 years
Born: Tennessee
Rank: Private (rifleman)
KIB

Robert McKinney came to Texas from New Orleans.

He may have been one of the volunteers who accompanied James Bowie to Bexar and the Alamo.

MELTON, ELIEL (1798–3/6/1836)
Age: 38 years (merchant)
Born: Georgia
Residence: Nashville-on-the-Brazos, Texas
Rank: Lieutenant (quartermaster, staff officer)
KIB

Eliel Melton was the son of Jonathan and Tibatha Melton. He was single when he came to Texas and registered to reside in Nacogdoches on 1/25/1830.

He made his living as a merchant, in business with Joseph L. Hood.

Melton took part in the siege and battle of Bexar and remained in Bexar, serving as quartermaster to the garrison.

Susannah Dickerson, in giving an account of the Alamo battle, described a defender vaulting the wall where it was lowest. She gave his name as "Milton."[92]

Several of the Alamo defenders were slain outside the walls. It is quite possible that Eliel Melton was one of them.[93]

MILLER, THOMAS R. (1795–3/6/1836)
Age: 41 years (town clerk of the Gonzales City Council,
  general store owner and farmer)
Born: Tennessee
Residence: Gonzales, Texas
Rank: Private (rifleman, Gonzales Ranging Company)
KIB

Thomas R. Miller was married to Sidney Gaston (1816–1838) by bond on 3/11/1832. They had one child who died in infancy, and the couple separated on 7/22/1833.

During 1834, Miller's house served as the meeting place of the Gonzales Town Council. He was reportedly the wealthiest resident of Gonzales at the time.

For the period of November 3–14, 1835, he served as a member of the Texas Consultation.[94]

Miller was one of the original "Old Eighteen" defenders of the Gonzales cannon. He rode to the Alamo as a member of the Gonzales Ranging Company, arriving there on 3/1/1836.

He furnished supplies for the relief force from his store in Gonzales.

MILLS, WILLIAM (10/6/1815–3/6/1836)
Age: 21 years
Born: Chattanooga, Tennessee
Residence: Austin's Colony, Texas
Rank: Private (rifleman)
KIB

William Mills was the son of John and Martha Ewing

Mills. He immigrated to Texas from Adamsville, Madison County, Mississippi, in 1833.

He may have been one of the volunteers who accompanied James Bowie to Bexar and the Alamo.

MILLSAPS, ISAAC (1795–3/6/1836)
Age: 41 years
Born: Mississippi
Residence: Gonzales, Texas
Rank: Private (rifleman, Gonzales Ranging Company)
KIB

Isaac Millsaps was the son of William and Rebecca Webster Millsaps.

His wife Mary was blind, and they had seven young children.

On 2/23/1836, Millsaps was mustered into service as a member of the Gonzales Ranging Company. He entered the Alamo with this unit on 3/1/1836.

A letter, believed to have been written by Millsaps while in the Alamo, has recently been found to be a forgery.[95]

MITCHASSON, EDWARD F. (1806–3/6/1836)
Age: 30 years (doctor)
Born: Virginia
Residence: Washington County, Texas
Rank: Possibly surgeon
KIB

Edward F. Mitchasson came to Texas from either Missouri or Mississippi.

He entered the service as a private in Captain Edwards's company on 11/30/1835.

He was severely wounded in the battle of Bexar, and it is not known whether he was able to play an active role in the Alamo battle.

On 1/1/1836 he was listed as a member of Captain Chenoweth's company.

Some lists give his rank as surgeon. It is possible, but it is not known definitely, if he served the garrison in that capacity.

His name is sometimes listed as "Mitcherson" or "Mitchson."

MITCHELL, EDWIN T. (1806–3/6/1836)
Age: 30 years
Rank: Private (rifleman, Captain White's infantry company)
KIB

Edwin T. Mitchell took part in the siege and battle of Bexar. He remained in Bexar as an infantryman in the Bexar Guards.

Either he or Napoleon B. Mitchell was bayonetted during the Alamo battle while trying to protect Juana Alsbury.

His brother, Dewarren Mitchell, died in the Goliad executions.

MITCHELL, NAPOLEON B. (1804–3/6/1836)
Age: 32 years
Rank: Private (artilleryman, Captain Carey's artillery
  company)
KIB

Napoleon B. Mitchell was the son of Asa and Emily (Brisband) Mitchell.

He took part in the siege and battle of Bexar and remained in Bexar as a member of Carey's company.

Either he or Edwin T. Mitchell was bayonetted during the Alamo battle while trying to protect Juana Alsbury.

MOORE, ROBERT B. (1781–3/6/1836)
Age: 55 years
Born: Martinsburg, Virginia
Rank: Private (rifleman, Captain Blazeby's infantry
  company)
KIB

Robert B. Moore's parents were from Ireland. Their name was O'Moore when they immigrated to America.

Moore came to Texas by way of New Orleans as a member of Breece's New Orleans Greys.

He took part in the siege and battle of Bexar and remained in Bexar as a member of Blazeby's company.

Robert was a cousin of Alamo defender Willis A. Moore.

MOORE, WILLIS A. (1808–3/6/1836)
Age: 28 years
Residence: Raymond, Mississippi
Rank: Private (rifleman)
KIB

Willis A. Moore came to Texas via Arkansas.

He joined the Texas army at Bexar on 11/26/1835 and took part in the siege and battle of Bexar. On 1/1/1836 he joined Captain Chenoweth's company.

Moore was a cousin of Alamo defender Robert B. Moore.

On muster rolls his name is given simply as "Moore."

MUSSELMAN, ROBERT (1805–3/6/1836)
Age: 31 years (former United States soldier)
Born: Ohio
Residence: Pennsylvania
Rank: Sergeant (company NCO, Captain Blazeby's infantry company)
KIB

Robert Musselman was the son of Peter Musselman of Shelby County, Ohio.

He was a veteran of the United States Army, having served in the Seminole Indian War in Florida.

While Musselman was on active duty in Florida, his father died, leaving him little or no inheritance. He traveled to New Orleans and enlisted in the service of Texas as a sergeant in Breece's New Orleans Greys.

He took part in the siege and battle of Bexar and remained in Bexar as a sergeant in Blazeby's company.

Attorney Juan de Cordova of Galveston administered Musselman's estate, and in 1851, three land certificates were administered to him for a total of 4,036 acres.

NAVA, ANDRES (1810–3/6/1836)

Age: 26 years
Born: San Antonio de Bexar, Texas
Residence: Same
Rank: Private (rifleman, Captain Seguin's cavalry company)
KIB

Andres Nava was one of the native Texans enlisted for six months of service under the command of Juan Seguin.

He took part in the siege and battle of Bexar and returned to Bexar in Seguin's company.

After the battle of the Alamo, Demasio de los Reyes, who was ordered into the Alamo to remove bodies to be burned, recognized Nava's body in the ruins. He later swore to the fact that he knew Nava and recognized him there.

On 11/22/1860 Nava's half brother, Carmel Gonzara, and sister, Dorotea Munis, swore in an application for a land grant that Nava died at the Alamo. On 3/25/1861 a note was placed in their file stating that they were too poor to carry their claim any further.

NAVARRO, GERTRUDIS (1821–?)

Age: 15 years
Residence: San Antonio de Bexar, Texas
Rank: Civilian (noncombatant)
Survived the Alamo battle

Gertrudis Navarro was the daughter of José Angel Navarro II and younger sister of Juana Navarro de Alsbury. She and her sister were reared by the Veramendi family of San Antonio de Bexar.

Gertrudis entered the Alamo with her sister and her nephew, Alijo Perez, Jr., and was present with them throughout the entire Alamo siege and battle.

In later life, Gertrudis married Juan M. Cantu, a wealthy and influential Mexican. She lived out her life in Mexico.

NEGGAN, GEORGE (1808–3/6/1836)
Age: 28 years
Born: South Carolina
Residence: Gonzales, Texas
Rank: Private (rifleman, Gonzales Ranging Company)
KIB

George Neggan joined the relief force from Gonzales when it rode to the Alamo, arriving on 3/1/1836.

His heirs received the first bounty warrant in his name on 3/25/1851. They received five more acres in Smith County, Texas on 6/25/1918.

NELSON, ANDREW M. (1809–3/6/1836)
Age: 27 years
Born: Tennessee
Rank: Private (rifleman)
KIB

Andrew M. Nelson was the son of John and Elizabeth Mansfield Nelson. He was a single man.

Not much is known of this defender other than that he is one of three "Nelsons" on lists of Alamo defenders.

NELSON, EDWARD (1816–3/6/1836)
Age: 20 years
Residence: South Carolina
Rank: Private (rifleman, possibly Captain Baker's company)
KIB

Edward Nelson was the son of William Nelson.

He joined the army at Bexar on 11/26/1835 and took part in the siege and battle of Bexar as a member of Captain Peacock's artillery company. On 1/1/1836 he joined Captain Chenoweth's company. John Chenoweth later claimed one-third league of land as Nelson's administrator.

Edward Nelson may have been one of the volunteers who accompanied James Bowie to the Alamo.

Edward was the younger brother of Alamo defender George Nelson.

NELSON, GEORGE (1805–3/6/1836)
Age: 31 years
Residence: South Carolina
Rank: Private (rifleman, Captain Blazeby's infantry
  company)
KIB

George Nelson was the son of William Nelson and older brother of Alamo defender Edward Nelson.

He came to Texas by way of New Orleans as a member of Breece's New Orleans Greys.

George was wounded in the battle of Bexar and remained in Bexar as a member of Blazeby's company.

His name is sometimes listed as "H. G." or "H. J. Nelson."

NOBLES, BENJAMIN F.
Rank: Lieutenant (company officer, Captain Dimmit's
  company)
Left Alamo on 2/23/1836

Benjamin F. Nobles was a member of the Texan force at Guadalupe Victoria and a signer of the Collinsworth agreement on 10/9/1835.

During the taking of Goliad in early November 1835, Nobles and a squad of ten men were responsible for guarding one of two passes on the Nueces River.

Nobles served on the committee which prepared a preamble and resolutions in support of Philip Dimitt. He also signed the controversial Goliad Declaration on 12/20/1835.

Nobles rode to Bexar and the Alamo as a member of Captain Dimitt's company. On 2/23/1836 he accompanied Captain Dimitt from the Alamo to reconnoiter the Mexican army. He then left Bexar along with Dimitt.

Benjamin Nobles later served as an aid and courier for General Houston. On 4/4/1836 he was ordered by Houston to go with Harvey Hall and Daniel Kinchenoe and range between Mill Creek and the Colorado River to observe the movements of the Mexican army and report any findings to Houston.

After the battle of San Jacinto, Nobles went on furlough from the Texan army.

NONCOMBATANTS

Besides the noncombatants whose biographies are given in this work, there were also an undetermined number of other civilians who were in the Alamo during the siege and battle.

Joe, Travis's slave, mentioned other Negroes in the fort. He also mentioned one woman killed. He remembered seeing her body lying between two cannon.

Enrique Esparza recalled a Mrs. Victoriana and her family of several girls. He also remembered Juana Melton, wife of defender Eliel Melton, who may have been the sister of defender Toribio Losoya. Esparza mentioned Concepcion Losoya and her son Juan as being in the Alamo. They were probably the mother and brother of Toribio Losoya.[96]

NORTHCROSS, JAMES (1804–3/6/1836)
Age: 32 years (Methodist minister)
Born: Virginia
Residence: Bastrop, Texas
Rank: Private (artilleryman, Captain Carey's artillery company)
KIB

James Northcross was in Texas as early as 1831. On 4/22/1835 he registered in Milam County.

After the death of his first wife, he married Sarah Parrent Jenkins, the widow of Edward Jenkins, in 1835. They reared one son, besides Sarah's three children.

Northcross was a member of Captain Coleman's company during the Grass Fight.

He took part in the siege and battle of Bexar and remained in Bexar as a member of Carey's artillery company.

86

NOWLAN, JAMES (1809–3/6/1836)
Age: 27 years
Born: England
Residence: Same
Rank: Private (rifleman)
KIB

James Nowlan probably came to Texas as a member of Captain Cooke's company of New Orleans Greys. The name "James Nolind" is listed on the roster of Cooke's company.

He took part in the siege and battle of Bexar and was severely wounded in the battle. It is unlikely that he was able to play an active part in the Alamo battle.

OURY, WILLIAM SANDERS (8/13/1817–3/31/1887)
Age: 18 years
Born: Abingdon, Virginia
Residence: Texas
Rank: Private (rifleman/courier)
Left Alamo as a courier 2/29/1836

William S. Oury was the oldest of nine children of Augustus Oury, a landowner and planter. He came to Texas in 1833, instead of settling with his family in Missouri.

Oury was sent from the Alamo as a courier on or about 2/29/1836. He later served as a courier for General Houston and took part in the battle of San Jacinto.

On 11/6/1836 he enlisted in Captain Irwin's company of the 1st Infantry, Texan army, as a third corporal.

On 8/15/1838 a survey of 640 acres of land was made in Oury's name, in Polk County, Texas, for his military service. Oury, however, never followed up on the proper paperwork and the land was forfeited.

In December 1842 he served as a member of the ill-fated Mier Expedition against the Mexican town of the same name. When the expedition was captured and forced to draw lots (in this case black or white beans) to see who of their number would be executed, William Oury was one of the fortunate ones who picked a white bean and was spared.

He served in the Mexican War with the Texas Rangers

from 9/28/1845 to 3/28/1846 and then 6/29/1846 to 9/29/1846, and took part in the battle of Monterrey.

After the war he acquired a farm along the San Antonio River in Bexar. His family, from Missouri, joined him there in 1848 but returned to Missouri within a year.

In 1849 Oury married nineteen-year-old Inez Garcia of Durango, Mexico. He and his wife left Texas for California in the gold rush excitement. They remained in California until 1856, when they moved to Tucson, Arizona.

Oury became a cattle rancher and a well-respected citizen and community leader in Arizona. In 1857 he became an agent for the Butterfield Overland Stage Company and was also elected sheriff of Tucson several times.

On 4/30/1871 he was one of the leaders of the unfortunate and scandalous Camp Grant Massacre of Apache Indians, a raid that was allegedly mounted in retaliation for Apache depredations against settlers.

William Oury died at his home in Tucson on 3/31/1887 at age sixty-nine.

PAGAN, GEORGE (1810–3/6/1836)
Age: 26 years
Rank: Private
KIB

George Pagan came to Texas from Natchez, Mississippi.

He took part in the siege and battle of Bexar as a member of Neill's command.

Pagan received no bounty or land donations for his service.

PARKER, CHRISTOPHER ADAMS (1814–3/6/1836)
Age: 22 years
Residence: Vehlein's Colony, Texas
Rank: Private (rifleman, possibly Captain Dimitt's company)
KIB

Christopher A. Parker was the son of William and Hannah Armstrong Parker and was a single man.

He was a descendant of the Sparrow family, English

Quakers who had immigrated to Ireland during the Cromwell Protectorate. An ancestor, Samuel Sparrow, fought in Emmett's Rebellion and was expelled from Ireland.

Christopher's father fought in the Battle of New Orleans in 1814. His grandfather, James Armstrong, served under George Washington at Valley Forge.[97]

Christopher Parker came to Texas from Natchez, Mississippi, and registered in Vehlein's Colony on 11/20/1835.

He may have been one of the volunteers who accompanied Philip Dimitt to Bexar and the Alamo.

PARKS, WILLIAM (1805–3/6/1836)
Age: 31 years
Born: Rowan County, North Carolina
Residence: Austin's Colony, Texas
Rank: Private (rifleman, Captain White's infantry company)
KIB

William Parks was the son of Jonathan and Catherine Turner Parks.

He took part in the siege and battle of Bexar and remained in Bexar as a member of the Bexar Guards.

PATTON, WILLIAM HESTER (1808–6/12/1842)
Age: 28 years (merchant, surveyor)
Born: Hopkinsville, Kentucky
Residence: Brazoria County, Texas
Rank: Captain (commanding officer of a small company/
  courier)
Left Alamo probably as a courier

William H. Patton came to Texas in 1828, settling in what is now Brazoria County. In 1832 he took part in the battle of Velasco against Mexican forces.[98]

Patton joined the Texan forces at the outbreak of the Texas Revolution and commanded a company in the siege and battle of Bexar. Only ten or twelve of his men followed him into town during the battle.

On 12/21/1835 Patton was ordered by Sam Houston to

Velasco to act as assistant quartermaster general to organize and direct the volunteer troops arriving in Texas by sea. These orders were probably rescinded or not followed through, since on 1/17/1836, Houston stated in a letter that he believed William Patton was in Bexar and he expected him to return to La Vaca County with a company of men as soon as possible.[99]

Apparently, Patton was under similar orders to those issued to Capt. Philip Dimitt. He was to remain in Bexar if it was invested, and to fall back if it was not.

According to Dr. John Sutherland, who accompanied Patton to Bexar with ten others, their company did not reach Bexar until 1/18/1836.[100]

Patton remained in Bexar as an officer of the garrison, and was still there as late as 2/5/1836. The exact date of his departure is not known, but it was probably just before or just after the arrival of the Mexican troops.

He joined Houston and commanded a company of his army, and also served as an aide-de-camp to Houston during the battle of San Jacinto.

Patton continued to serve the Texan army until 8/26/1837. He was part of the group which accompanied Santa Anna to Washington before his return to Mexico. Patton also served as quartermaster general of the army.

After Texan independence, he settled on the San Antonio River, thirty-five miles south of San Antonio. He served in the second congress of Texas, representing Bexar County.

William Patton was murdered on 6/12/1842 by a band of Mexicans.[101]

PEREZ, ALEJO, JR. (1834–?)
Age: 18 months
Residence: San Antonio de Bexar, Texas
Rank: Civilian (noncombatant, son of Juana Navarro de
    Alsbury)
Survived the Alamo battle

Alejo Perez, Jr., was the son of Alejo Perez, Sr., and Juana Navarro de Alsbury, formerly Mrs. Perez.

He was brought into the Alamo by his mother and aunt, Gertrudis Navarro. Although he was present during the entire siege and battle of the Alamo, this infant has virtually been forgotten by history.

Alejo Perez, Jr., was still living in San Antonio in 1900.[102]

PERRY, RICHARDSON (1817–3/6/1836)
Age: 19 years
Born: Texas
Residence: Brazos County, Texas
Rank: Private (artilleryman, Captain Carey's artillery
    company)
KIB

Richardson Perry was the son of Burwell Perry, an early settler of Texas.

He was a single man and received an original land grant in Brazos County, Texas, on 10/10/1835.

He took part in the siege and battle of Bexar and remained in Bexar as a member of Carey's company.

POLLARD, AMOS (10/29/1803–3/6/1836)
Age: 32 years (doctor)
Born: Ashburnham, Massachusetts
Residence: Gonzales, Texas
Rank: Regimental surgeon (chief surgeon, staff officer)
KIB

Amos Pollard was the son of Jonas and Martha Martin Westminister Pollard. He grew up in Surry, New Hampshire, and was a graduate of the Vermont Academy in Castletown, Vermont, in 1825 with a degree in medicine.[103]

He lived for a time in Greenbush, New York, and then spent the years 1828–1834 practicing medicine at various locations in Manhattan.

He married Fanny Oeela and they had one daughter. Very little is known about his wife, and it is uncertain when and where they married.

Pollard left Manhattan for Texas at a time when abolitionist riots and cholera epidemics were sweeping the city. He traveled to New Orleans, and some sources indicate that he may have left his wife and child there while he traveled to Texas and settled in Gonzales.

Pollard took part in the fight for the Gonzales cannon and marched on Bexar as a private in Captain York's volunteer company.

On 10/23/1835 he was appointed surgeon of the regiment by Stephen F. Austin.

After the battle of Bexar it was Pollard's responsibility to care for the sick and wounded of the garrison. He remained in Bexar as chief surgeon on the staff of Colonel Neill. He retained this position during the Alamo siege and battle.

Amos Pollard probably died defending the Alamo's two-story hospital building along with the sick and wounded.

Several letters written by him during the occupation of Bexar give a good picture of the conditions in Bexar at the time.

A portrait of Pollard was painted sometime before he immigrated to Texas. He is the only Alamo victim, other than Travis, Bowie, and Crockett, of whom a portrait was done from life. A copy of his likeness is on display in the Alamo today.

REYNOLDS, JOHN PURDY (3/7/1806–3/6/1836)
Age: 29 years (doctor)
Born: Cedar Springs, Mifflin County, Pennsylvania
Residence: Mifflin County, Pennsylvania
Rank: Private (rifleman, Captain Harrison's company,
   VAC)
KIB

John P. Reynolds was the son of Judge David and Mary Purdy Reynolds. He was a graduate of Jefferson Medical College, Philadelphia, class of 1827, and practiced medicine for seven years in Mifflin County.

Reynolds traveled to Texas in 1835 with Alamo defender William McDowell. They were sworn into the Volunteer Auxiliary Corps of Texas at Nacogdoches before Judge Forbes on 1/14/1836.

Reynolds joined Harrison's company and arrived at Bexar with this group on or about 2/9/1836. He served as a private during the Alamo siege and battle, and it is unknown whether or not he was utilized as a surgeon.

His medical books are on display in the Alamo today.

ROBERTS, THOMAS H. (?–3/6/1836)
Rank: Private (rifleman, possibly Captain Baker's company)
KIB

Thomas H. Roberts joined Captain Chenoweth's company on 1/13/1836.

He may have been one of the volunteers who accompanied James Bowie to Bexar and the Alamo.

ROBERTSON, JAMES WATERS (2/18/1812–3/6/1836)
Age: 24 years
Born: Tennessee
Rank: Private (rifleman)
KIB

James W. Robertson was the son of Felix and Lydia Waters Robertson. He was married to Sarah Carson.

James came to Texas from Louisiana and took part in the siege and battle of Bexar. It is uncertain as to what unit he belonged to during the Alamo siege and battle.

ROBINSON (1808–3/6/1836)
Age: 28 years
Born: Scotland
Rank: 4th Sergeant (company NCO, Captain Carey's
  artillery company)
KIB

Isaac Robinson came to Texas from Louisiana.

He took part in the siege and battle of Bexar and remained in Bexar as a member of Carey's artillery company.

Robinson's name has been listed as "Isaac," but the Isaac Robinson referred to was still living after the Alamo battle.

ROSE, JAMES M. (1805–3/6/1836)
Age: 31 years
Born: Ohio
Residence: Arkansas
Rank: Private (rifleman)
KIB

James M. Rose was the son of Dr. Robert Henry and Frances Taylor Madison Rose. He was the nephew of James Madison, the fourth president of the United States.

On 6/30/1857 Susannah Dickerson agreed before Samuel J. R. McDowell, the county court clerk of Caldwell, Texas, that James Rose joined "the late David Crockett to engage in the war between Mexico and Texas." She also agreed that he and Crockett were on friendly terms.[104]

She described Rose as being between thirty-five and forty years old and "of medium height, heavy set, rather full square face, very quick spoken."[105] On another occasion she described him as being thirty years old, medium height, with light freckled skin, light sandy hair, blue-gray eyes, broad, stooped shoulders, and weighing between 150 and 160 pounds.[106]

Susannah Dickerson saw James often during the siege and "upon one occasion he and my husband Capt. Dickinson, spoke of a narrow escape Rose had made from a Mexican officer after that first attack."[107]

ROSE, LOUIS (5/11/1785–1850)
Age: 50 years (former French soldier, sawmill worker,
  teamster)
Born: Laferee, Ardennes, France
Residence: Nacogdoches, Texas
Rank: Private (rifleman, possibly Captain Baker's company)
Left Alamo sometime between 3/3 and 3/6/1836

Louis Rose, sometimes called "Moses" Rose, had been a noncommissioned officer in Napoleon Bonaparte's army. He took part in the Russian campaign and the retreat from Moscow.

He immigrated to Texas and settled in Nacogdoches,

probably in 1827, buying land west of the Angelina River. In 1835 he sold his farm, borrowed money, and left his home to fight in the Texas Revolution.

Rose fought in the siege and battle of Bexar in Capt. Thomas J. Rusk's company. He may have been one of the volunteers who accompanied James Bowie to Bexar and the Alamo. He was present during the siege of the Alamo, but left before the final battle. During his escape, Rose's legs sustained many wounds from cacti and thorns. They became infected and he grew sick and feverish. He made his way to the home of the Zuber family in Grimes County and recuperated there.[108]

After the Texas Revolution, Rose returned to Nacogdoches and opened a meat market.

He was said to have a violent and surly attitude and became involved in a number of violent incidents. In 1837 he was called as a witness in a murder trial. One year later he almost became a murder victim himself, when he was slashed by a drunken knife wielder. On one occasion, Rose reportedly chased a man from his shop with a shotgun, and on another occasion he slashed a man with a knife because he complained about the quality of meat Rose sold.

In the early 1840s, Rose left Texas and drifted to Natchitoches, Louisiana, finally settling at the home of Aaron Ferguson, near Logansport.

In later life he still suffered a great deal from the chronic leg sores sustained on his flight from the Alamo.

If ever he was asked why he did not remain at the Alamo with the rest, it is said that he would always reply, "By God, I wasn't ready to die."[109]

He died in 1850 and is buried in an unmarked grave near Logansport.

Years after the Alamo battle, an aged Susannah Dickerson recalled that one man chose to escape from the Alamo. She remembered his name as "Ross."[110]

RUSK, JACKSON J. (?–3/6/1836)
Born: Ireland
Residence: Nacogdoches, Texas

Rank: Private (rifleman, possibly Captain Baker's company)
KIB

Jackson J. Rusk registered in Zavala's Colony on 9/30/1835, but title was never completed.

He may have been one of the volunteers who accompanied James Bowle to Bexar and the Alamo.

No heirs ever claimed the lands entitled to him after his death.

RUTHERFORD, JOSEPH (1798–3/6/1836)
Age: 38 years
Born: Kentucky
Residence: Nacogdoches, Texas
Rank: Private (artilleryman, Captain Carey's artillery
  company)
KIB

Joseph Rutherford was the son of Julius and Rhoda Rutherford. He was a married man with a daughter who was later reared by Joseph Durst.

He took part in the siege and battle of Bexar and received a donation certificate for 640 acres of land for his service. He remained in Bexar as a member of Carey's company.

RYAN, ISAAC (3/1/1805–3/6/1836)
Age: 31 years
Born: St. Landry Parish, Louisiana
Residence: Opelousas, Louisiana
Rank: Private (rifleman, Captain White's infantry company)
KIB

Isaac Ryan was the son of Jacob and Marie Hartgrove Ryan.

He took part in the siege and battle of Bexar and remained in Bexar as a member of the Bexar Guards.

SAUCEDO, TRINIDAD (1809–?)
Age: 27 years (servant)
Residence: San Antonio de Bexar, Texas
Rank: Civilian (noncombatant)
Left Alamo sometime before the final battle.

Trinidad Saucedo had once been a servant in the household of the Veramendi family, the in-laws of James Bowie.[111]

She may have accompanied Juana Alsbury and Gertrudis Navarro into the Alamo, or she may have come in under the protection of James Bowie.

Years later, Enrique Esparza stated that Trinidad left the Alamo during a three-day armistice in the siege.

SCURLOCK, MIAL (5/25/1803 or 1809–3/6/1836)
Age: 27–33 years
Born: Chatham County, North Carolina
Residence: San Augustine, Texas
Rank: Private (rifleman)
KIB

Mial Scurlock was the son of Joseph and Martha Jones Glasgow Scurlock. He lived for a time in Tennessee and Mississippi.

In 1834 he came to Texas with his brother and their slaves, by way of Louisiana, settling in San Augustine.

Scurlock volunteered for service in the Texan army on 10/17/1835 and took part in the siege and battle of Bexar.

SEGUIN, JUAN NEPOMUCENO (10/27/1806–1890)
Age: 29 years (rancher, political chief of Bexar)
Born: San Antonio de Bexar, Texas
Residence: Seguin Ranch, south of Bexar
Rank: Captain (commanding officer of cavalry company/
   courier)
Left the Alamo on 2/25/1836 to rally reinforcements

Juan N. Seguin, the son of Juan José Maria Erasmo de Jesus and Josefa Becerra Seguin, was one of the most influential citizens in Texas. He was the political leader of Bexar and an opponent of Santa Anna.

At the outbreak of the Texas Revolution, Seguin raised a company of volunteers from Bexar and the ranches along the San Antonio River. He took part in the battle of Concepcion and the siege and battle of Bexar.

In January 1836 Juan was commissioned captain in the regular Texas cavalry, and with his company he joined Travis's command.

Seguin and his men entered the Alamo on 2/23/1836 with the rest of the garrison when the Mexican army took possession of Bexar.

On 2/25/1836 Seguin and one of his men, Antonio Cruz y Arocha, left the Alamo under orders from Travis to rally reinforcements to the Alamo.

After making his way through the Mexican lines, Seguin managed to gather a company of twenty-five men. They were joined by a group of twelve men under Dr. John Sutherland, who had left the Alamo as a courier on 2/23/1836, and Dr. Horace Alsbury, whose wife, Juana, was in the Alamo. By 2/28/1836 they were waiting on the Cibolo River, hoping to link up with the force under Colonel Fannin. Fannin failed to march, and the Alamo fell before Seguin's meager force could reach it.

During the "Runaway Scrape,"[112] Juan Seguin commanded the rear guard of the Texan army, insuring that no Texan families were left in the path of Santa Anna's army. He was also instrumental in preventing the Mexican army from crossing the Brazos River and overtaking the Texan force.

On 4/21/1836 Seguin took part in the battle of San Jacinto as the commander of the 9th company, 2nd regiment.

In May of that year he was promoted to lieutenant colonel and ordered to take over Bexar until the civil government could be restored. In 1837 he organized and supervised a ceremony in Bexar in which the remains of some of the Alamo defenders were buried. He also prevented Bexar from being destroyed by orders of Gen. Felix Huston, who feared the city could not be defended in case of another Mexican invasion.

From 1838 to 1840, Seguin served in the Senate of Texas. In 1841 he was elected mayor of San Antonio.

His popularity as a leader began to slip when his views came in conflict with those of newer Texas settlers from the United States.

In 1842 Seguin was forced to leave Texas due to trumped-up charges that he was aiding Mexican forces which were reinvading Texas, and also due to numerous threats against his life.[113] He traveled to Mexico with the intention of joining relatives in Saltillo.

He was imprisoned at Laredo, by the Mexicans, and freed by Santa Anna only after he agreed to help lead Mexican troops under General Woll into Texas to seize Bexar in September 1842.

Seguin returned to Mexico after only one month in Texas. He did not return permanently to Texas until after the Mexican-American War.

Juan Seguin lived out the remainder of his life in Texas, but his trust and political career had been ruined by the unjust events of 1842.

He died in Nuevo Laredo in 1890 and was buried there. His remains were disinterred several years ago and buried in Seguin, Texas, a final homecoming for this heroic but tragic figure of the Texas Revolution.

SEWELL, MARCUS L. (1805–3/6/1836)
Age: 31 years (shoemaker)
Born: England
Residence: Gonzales, Texas
Rank: Private (rifleman, Gonzales Ranging Company)
KIB

Marcus L. Sewell came to Texas by way of New Orleans and settled in Gonzales.

On 2/23/1836 he was mustered into service as a member of the Gonzales Ranging Company. He rode to the Alamo with this group, arriving on 3/1/1836.

SHIED, MANSON (1811–3/6/1836)
Age: 25 years (carpenter)
Born: Georgia

Residence: Brazoria
Rank: Private (artilleryman, Captain Carey's artillery
  company)
KIB

Manson Shied took part in the siege and battle of Bexar and remained in Bexar as a member of Carey's company.

His heirs were entitled to a land grant of 640 acres and later 1,280 acres. Both grants were later sold for a mere pittance. (The 640 acres sold for $54.30.)

SIMMONS, CLEVELAND KINLOCH (6/8/1815–3/6/1836)
Age: 20 years
Born: Charleston, South Carolina
Residence: Same
Rank: 1st Lieutenant (company officer, Captain Forsyth's
  cavalry company)
KIB

Cleveland K. Simmons was the son of William and Sarah Clifford Young Simmons of Charleston, South Carolina. He traveled to Texas in January 1836 aboard the schooner *Santiago,* along with Alamo defender Richard W. Ballentine.

He was commissioned a lieutenant in the regular Texas cavalry by Governor Henry Smith before leaving San Felipe for Bexar.

He traveled to Bexar and the Alamo as an officer of Forsyth's cavalry company, arriving on or about 2/2/1836.

SMITH, ANDREW H. (1815–3/6/1836)
Age: 21 years
Rank: Private (rifleman, possibly Captain Forsyth's cavalry
  company)
KIB?

Andrew H. Smith came to Texas from Tennessee.

He is carried on many of the various lists of Alamo victims, but there is a possibility that his name was incorrectly included.

In his letter of 1/28/1836 to Governor Henry Smith,

Travis lists six men who deserted from Forsyth's company. Among those listed is Andrew Smith. The letter states that he deserted with "a sorrel horse, saddle, & bridle — blanket gun and shot pouch."[114]

There are several possible explanations concerning Smith's inclusion on Alamo rosters:

1) Since Andrew Smith is a fairly common name, the deserter and the Alamo victim may have been two distinct people;

2) Andrew Smith could have deserted and then showed up at Bexar and the Alamo later on. Alfonso Steele, who is also listed as a deserter in the same letter, later took part in the battle of San Jacinto.

It is possible that Andrew Smith did desert and for years he has been incorrectly listed as an Alamo victim.

SMITH, CHARLES S. (1806–3/6/1836)
Age: 30 years
Born: Maryland
Rank: Private (artilleryman, Captain Carey's artillery company)
KIB

Charles S. Smith was the son of Charles Somerset and Ann Sothern Smith. He came to Texas from Louisiana.

Smith entered the service of Texas on 10/10/1835 and took part in the siege and battle of Bexar as a member of Captain Parrott's artillery company.

On 12/14/1835 he volunteered to serve four more months and remained in Bexar as a member of Carey's artillery company.

Colonel Neill later stated of Charles Smith that he "served faithfully and fell in the Alamo."[115]

Thomas Kenny, the administrator of Smith's estate, collected Smith's pay account of $74.66 on 10/12/1837.

SMITH, JOHN WILLIAM (3/4/1792–1/12/1845)
Age: 44 years (civil engineer, carpenter, boardinghouse keeper)
Born: Virginia

Residence: San Antonio de Bexar, Texas
Rank: Storekeeper (scout/courier/guide)
Left Alamo as a courier on 3/3/1836

John W. Smith moved to Texas in 1826 from Hannibal, Missouri. He settled in Bexar and in 1831 married Maria de Jesus Curbelo.

Smith was taken prisoner by the Mexican troops in Bexar when the Texan army besieged the town in November 1835. He managed to escape from the town and was instrumental in drawing maps and plans for the Texan assault on Bexar. After the battle of Bexar he remained in the town, serving the garrison as storekeeper.

On 2/23/1836 he and Dr. John Sutherland volunteered to ride out of Bexar to confirm a sentry's report that the Mexican army was approaching. Their rapid return alerted the garrison, which quickly fell back to the protection of the Alamo.

When Smith arrived at the Alamo later on, he was sent by Travis to spread the word of the Mexican army's arrival. Outside of town he again joined up with Dr. Sutherland, who had also been sent out as a courier.

Smith returned to the Alamo on 3/1/1836 as the scout and guide for the Gonzales Ranging Company. He was sent from the Alamo again on 3/3/1836, carrying some of the last letters and communications with him. He was again returning to the Alamo from San Felipe with twenty-five volunteers when the Alamo fell on 3/6/1836.

After Texan independence, John Smith was elected mayor of San Antonio three times. During the Mexican invasion of 1842, he was instrumental in gathering intelligence information for the Texans. Unfortunately, Smith became a bitter opponent of fellow Alamo defender, Juan N. Seguin, and according to Seguin, became part of the conspiracy to ruin him.

After serving as mayor of San Antonio, Smith served as senator in the Texan Congress, representing Bexar County, until the time of his death.

He died of pneumonia in 1845 at Washington-on-the-Brazos, Texas.

He was described as a handsome, blue-eyed man, over six feet tall, with reddish brown hair.

SMITH, JOSHUA G. (1808–3/6/1836)
Age: 28 years
Born: North Carolina
Residence: Bastrop, Texas
Rank: Sergeant (company NCO, Captain Forsyth's cavalry
   company)
KIB

Joshua G. Smith left North Carolina for Texas and was never again heard of by his family.

In March 1835 he received a quarter league of land in Robertson County, Texas.

He traveled to Bexar and the Alamo as a sergeant in Captain Forsyth's company, arriving in Bexar on or about 2/2/1836.

Jesse Bartlett was the administrator of Smith's estate and received the balance of his pay, which amounted to $14.92, on 3/3/1837.

Susannah Dickerson described Joshua Smith as "a man of about five feet some inches height, spare made, dark eyes and complexion and appeared to be between 25 and 35 years of age."[116]

SMITH, WILLIAM H. (1811–3/6/1836)
Age: 25 years
Residence: Nacogdoches, Texas
Rank: Private (artilleryman, Captain Carey's artillery
   company)
KIB

William H. Smith served in the Texan army for six months prior to and including the Alamo siege.

He took part in the siege and battle of Bexar and remained in Bexar as a member of Carey's company.

SMITHER, LAUNCELOT (1800–9/11/1842)

Age: 36 years (horse trader, farmer, medic to the Mexican
   garrison at Bexar)
Residence: Austin's Colony, Texas
Rank: Private (courier)
Left Alamo on 2/23/1836, possibly as an official courier

Launcelot Smither came to Texas from Alabama in 1828.
He was granted a league of land on the Brazos River but never
farmed it. He spent most of his time in Bexar, trading horses
and for a time acting as an unofficial "doctor" for the Mexican garrison.

In September 1835 he accompanied the Mexican force
under Lt. Francisco Castañeda to Gonzales, acting as an inter-
mediary for the Mexicans in their attempt to repossess the
Gonzales cannon. During the negotiations, Smither was held
prisoner by the Texan commander, Col. John H. Moore, and
was not permitted to return to the Mexican camp.

Following the brief fight for the cannon, Smither remained in Gonzales when the Mexican troops returned to
Bexar. He started to accompany the Texan force under Stephen F. Austin on its march to Bexar but was ordered back to
Gonzales to repair damage to the home of Ezekiel Williams
caused by the fighting.

On 11/2/1835 Smither was severely beaten by a group of
volunteers passing through Gonzales, who robbed some of the
houses and generally terrorized the town's women. Susannah
Dickerson, who was driven from her home, asked Smither to
accompany her back. He did, and was dragged into the street
by the men who beat him "to a poltice." [117]

On 12/1/1835 the provisional government authorized
payment to him of $270 to cover lost property that was seized
by Lieutenant Castañeda and that which was taken from him
by the vandals at Gonzales.

From Gonzales, Smither traveled to San Felipe. Sometime between 1/8 and 2/23/1836 he made his way to Bexar,
possibly with the men who accompanied Travis. He left Bexar
on 2/23/1836 at approximately 4:00 P.M. and traveled to Gonzales to spread the word of the Mexican army's arrival. It is

uncertain whether he left on his own or under orders from Travis.

On 2/24/1836 Capt. Albert Martin passed along Travis's famous letter addressed to "The people of Texas and all Americans in the world" to Launcelot Smither at Gonzales.

Smither added his own note to the letter and left Gonzales to carry the message to San Felipe.

It is unknown if Smither made any attempt to return to the Alamo.

From 1839 to 1840, he served as the city treasurer of San Antonio. From 8/19 to 9/7/1841 he served as mayor pro-tempore of San Antonio during an absence of Juan N. Seguin.

He was killed on 9/11/1842, with three others, at Sutherland Springs by Mexican troops of General Woll's force.

SOWELL, ANDREW JACKSON (6/27/1815–1/4/1883)
Age: 20 years (farmer)
Born: Davidson County, Tennessee
Residence: Gonzales, Texas
Rank: Private (rifleman/courier)
Left Alamo as a courier, date unknown

Andrew J. Sowell was the son of John N. Sowell, Sr., of Tennessee. He moved with his family from Tennessee to Missouri and then to Texas, settling in Gonzales in 1829. In Gonzales he was the schoolmate of two other future Alamo defenders, John Gaston and Galba Fuqua.

In 1833 he and his brothers raised the first corn grown by white men in Guadalupe County.

During the Texas Revolution, Sowell took part in the fight for the Gonzales cannon, the battle of Concepcion, and the Grass Fight.

Sometime during the siege of the Alamo, he and Byrd Lockhart were ordered out to obtain supplies for the garrison. They were delayed in Gonzales, trying to buy cattle and supplies, and did not return to the Alamo before its fall.

Sowell left the Alamo so close to the time of the final battle that, for a time, it was believed he died there. His name was entered on the first Alamo monument.

After the Texas Revolution, Andrew Sowell had a long career with the Texas Rangers. He took part in the Mexican War and served in the Confederate army during the Civil War. He became a noted scout and friend of Kit Carson.

Sowell died in Seguin, Texas, at age sixty-eight and is buried in Mofield Cemetery.

Alamo defender Marcus L. Sewell was a cousin of Andrew's father.

STARR, RICHARD (1811–3/6/1836)
Age: 25 years
Born: England
Residence: Same
Rank: Private (rifleman, Captain Blazeby's infantry
  company)
KIB

Richard Starr came to Texas by way of New Orleans as a member of Breece's company of New Orleans Greys.

He took part in the siege and battle of Bexar and remained in Bexar as a member of Blazeby's company.

STEWART, JAMES E. (1808–3/6/1836)
Age: 28 years
Born: England
Rank: Private (rifleman)
KIB

Not much is known of defender James E. Stewart. His name is sometimes listed as "Stuart."

STOCKTON, RICHARD L. (1817–3/6/1836)
Age: 19 years
Born: Essex County, New Jersey
Residence: Virginia
Rank: Private (rifleman, Captain Harrison's company,
  VAC)
KIB

Richard L. Stockton traveled to Texas in 1835.

On 1/14/1836 he was sworn into the Volunteer Auxiliary Corps of Texas before Judge Forbes at Nacogdoches. He traveled to Bexar and the Alamo as a member of Harrison's company, arriving there on or about 2/9/1836.

SUMMERLIN, A. SPAIN (1817–3/6/1836)
Age: 19 years
Born: Tennessee
Residence: San Augustine, Texas
Rank: Private (rifleman, Captain White's infantry company)
KIB

A. Spain Summerlin, a single man, was the son of Thomas and Susan Summerlin. He and his family came to Texas from Arkansas and his parents settled in Nacogdoches.

Summerlin volunteered for the Texan army on 10/17/1835 and took part in the siege and battle of Bexar. He remained in Bexar as a member of the Bexar Guards.

SUMMERS, WILLIAM E. (1812–3/6/1836)
Age: 24 years
Born: Tennessee
Residence: Gonzales, Texas
Rank: Private (rifleman, Gonzales Ranging Company)
KIB

William E. Summers was mustered into service on 2/23/1836 as a member of the Gonzales Ranging Company. He rode to the relief of the Alamo with this group, arriving on 3/1/1836.

SUTHERLAND, JOHN (5/11/1792–4/11/1867)
Age: 43 years (doctor)
Born: Danville, Virginia
Residence: Tuscumbia, Alabama
Rank: Private (medical assistant/scout/courier, Captain
  Patton's company)
Left Alamo as a courier on 2/23/1836

John Sutherland was the son of John and Agnes Shelton

Sutherland. His father was a former officer in George Washington's army. His family moved from Virginia to Tennessee in 1805.

By 1824 Sutherland was living in Decatur, Alabama. He worked in the mercantile and banking businesses, eventually becoming bank president.

He took up the practice of medicine under what was known as the "Thomsonian" system, based on the practice of Samuel Thompson, involving the use of steam, lobelia, red peppers, vegetable compounds, and such.

He left Tuscumbia, Alabama, for Texas in late 1835, following his older brother, George Sutherland, who had moved there in 1830.

John Sutherland took the oath of allegiance to the provisional government of Texas at San Felipe in December 1835. He joined the company of Capt. William H. Patton and traveled to Bexar with ten other volunteers.

In Bexar he took up residence with Almeron Dickerson's family at the Musquiz house on the southwest corner of Portero Street and the Main Plaza. He aided Dr. Amos Pollard in caring for the sick and wounded of the garrison.

Sutherland described James Bowie's illness as "of a peculiar nature . . . not to be cured by an ordinary treatment."[118]

On the afternoon of 2/23/1836, Sutherland volunteered to go out as a scout when the Texan sentry, posted in the bell tower of the San Fernando Church, spotted the advance column of Mexican troops. He and John W. Smith rode out from Bexar and confirmed that the enemy troops were actually approaching the town. While galloping back to town, he sustained a painful injury to his knee when his horse fell on muddy ground.

Upon reaching Bexar, he found Captain Harrison's company guarding the town, and he was accompanied by David Crockett to report to Travis at the Alamo. Sutherland was ordered by Travis to serve as a courier, and later that afternoon he left the Alamo.

Outside of Bexar, he again joined up with John W. Smith and they rode together to Gonzales. Sutherland attempted to return to the Alamo with a small group of volunteers, but the Alamo fell before they were able to reach it.

For the remainder of the revolution, he served as courier, aide-de-camp, and private secretary to David G. Burnet.[119]

In 1837 Sutherland settled in Egypt, Texas, with his family, and practiced medicine. In 1840 he moved with his family to Wilson County, at the site of some sulfur springs on the Cibolo River. The site became known as Sutherland Springs, with John serving as postmaster.

In 1860 he wrote his "Account of the Fall of the Alamo," which was not published until seventy-six years later.

He was married three times and had several children. He died at the age of seventy-five at Sutherland Springs.

SUTHERLAND, WILLIAM DePRIEST (8/10/1818–3/6/1836)
Age: 17 years (medical student)
Residence: Navidad, Texas
Rank: Private (rifleman)
KIB

William D. Sutherland was the son of George and Frances Menefree Sutherland, and nephew of Dr. John Sutherland. He apparently stayed in Alabama with his uncle, attending LaGrange College in Tuscumbia, when his parents left for Texas in 1830.

William Sutherland was in Texas by 1835. He attended a meeting at the Navidad and La Vaca Rivers on 7/17/1835, calling for a consultation of Texas communities.[120]

He joined the garrison at Bexar on 1/18/1836, possibly arriving there with the group under Captain Patton.

TAYLOR, EDWARD (1812–3/6/1836)
Age: 24 years (farm hand)
Born: Tennessee
Residence: Liberty, Texas
Rank: Private (rifleman)
KIB

Edward Taylor was the son of Anson and Elizabeth

Maley Taylor, and the older brother of Alamo defenders George and James Taylor.

When the Texas Revolution broke out, he and his brothers were employed picking cotton for Captain Dorsett on his farm in Liberty, Texas. As soon as they finished their job, they left for the Texan army.

Although Taylor's age is usually given as twenty-four years, Captain Dorsett's daughter stated, years later, that he was twenty-one at the time.

TAYLOR, GEORGE (1816–3/6/1836)
Age: 20 years (farm hand)
Born: Tennessee
Residence: Liberty, Texas
Rank: Private (rifleman)
KIB

George Taylor was the son of Anson and Elizabeth Maley Taylor, and younger brother of Alamo defenders Edward and James Taylor.

He worked on the Dorsett farm with his brothers and left for the army with them.

His age is usually given as twenty years, but Captain Dorsett's daughter stated that he was fifteen at the time. This may have been due to an error on her part, or he actually was fifteen and lied about his age to enter the army.

TAYLOR, JAMES (1814–3/6/1836)
Age: 22 years (farm hand)
Born: Tennessee
Residence: Liberty, Texas
Rank: Private (rifleman)
KIB

James Taylor was the son of Anson and Elizabeth Maley Taylor and brother of Alamo defenders George and Edward Taylor.

He worked on the Dorsett farm with his brothers and joined the Texan army with them.

His age is usually given as twenty-two years, but Captain Dorsett's daughter stated that he was seventeen at the time.

A bronze sculpture of the Taylor brothers, created by Lincoln Borglum (son of Gutzon Borglum, the sculptor of Mt. Rushmore), stands in Abilene, Texas. Taylor County, Texas, is named for them.

TAYLOR, WILLIAM (1799–3/6/1836)
Age: 37 years
Born: Tennessee
Residence: Little River Community (now Milam County), Texas
Rank: Private (rifleman)
KIB

There were at least three William Taylors in the Texan army during the Texas Revolution.
This William died at the Alamo, but no bounty or donation lands were ever given for his service.

THOMAS, B. ARCHER M. (1818–3/6/1836)
Age: 18 years
Born: Kentucky
Residence: Logan County, Kentucky
Rank: Private (rifleman, Captain Harrison's company, VAC)
KIB

B. A. M. Thomas traveled to Texas with Daniel Cloud, Peter J. Bailey, William Fontleroy, and Joseph G. Washington.
He was sworn into the Volunteer Auxiliary Corps of Texas on 1/14/1836 before Judge Forbes at Nacogdoches.
He traveled to Bexar and the Alamo as a member of Captain Harrison's company, arriving on or about 2/9/1836.

THOMAS, HENRY (1811–3/6/1836)
Age: 25 years
Born: Germany
Residence: Same

Rank: Private (rifleman, Captain Blazeby's infantry
  company)
KIB

Henry Thomas came to Texas by way of New Orleans as
a member of Breece's New Orleans Greys. He took part in the
siege and battle of Bexar as a member of Blazeby's company.
There are no certificates granting land in this defender's
name.

THOMPSON, JESSE G. (1798–3/6/1836)
Age: 38 years
Born: Arkansas
Residence: Brazoria, Texas
Rank: Private (rifleman)
KIB

Jesse G. Thompson was the son of John and Grizell Ellis
Thompson. He was married to Patience Carr.
He enlisted in the service of Texas on 10/23/1835 and
served in Captain Seal's ranger company until discharged on
1/25/1836.
It is uncertain to which unit Jesse belonged during the
siege and battle of the Alamo.

THOMSON, JOHN W. (1807–3/6/1836)
Age: 29 years (doctor)
Born: North Carolina
Residence: Tennessee
Rank: Private (rifleman/possibly surgeon)
KIB

John W. Thomson was the son of William Russell and
Elizabeth Sabb Thomson.
He traveled to Texas in late 1835 and was sworn into the
Volunteer Auxiliary Corps on 1/14/1836 before Judge Forbes
at Nacogdoches.
He traveled to Washington-on-the-Brazos as a member
of Captain Gilmer's company. At Washington, Thomson left
the company and traveled to Bexar on his own.

Although possible, it is not known if he served the Alamo garrison in the capacity of surgeon.

THURSTON, JOHN M. (4/17/1812–3/6/1836)

Age: 23 years
Born: Pennsylvania
Rank: 2nd Lieutenant (company officer, Captain Forsyth's cavalry company)
KIB

John M. Thurston was the son of Thomas Whiting and Mary Dorsey Thurston. There is evidence that his real name was Mountjoy Luckett Thurston, but he used the first name, John, of a brother who died in infancy in 1811.

He came to Texas from Kentucky and was appointed a second lieutenant in the Texas cavalry on 12/21/1835.

On 1/17/1836 he received a voucher for delivering a thirty-six-pound keg of rifle powder to Capt. Philip Dimitt. On 1/31/1836 he signed this claim over to T. D. Hendrick.

Thurston came to Bexar and the Alamo as an officer of Captain Forsyth's company.

His name is sometimes written as "Thruston."

TRAMMEL, BURKE (1810–3/6/1836)

Age: 26 years
Born: Ireland
Residence: Tennessee
Rank: Private (artilleryman, Captain Carey's artillery company)
KIB

Burke Trammel took part in the siege and battle of Bexar and was issued a donation certificate for 640 acres of land for his service.

He remained in Bexar as a member of Carey's company.

His name is sometimes written as "Tommel."

TRAVIS, WILLIAM BARRET (8/9/1809–3/6/1836)

Age: 26 years (lawyer, newspaperman, teacher)
Born: Red Banks Church, South Carolina
Residence: San Felipe, Texas
Rank: Lieutenant colonel (commanding officer of the Alamo
  garrison)
KIB

William B. Travis was the son of Mark and Jemima Stall-worth Travis. Sometime between 1818 and 1820, his family moved from South Carolina to Conecuh County, Alabama. In Alabama, Travis studied law under Judge James Dellett of Clairborne.

On 10/28/1828 Travis married Rosanna Cato. They had two children, Charles Edward and Susan Isabelle. The Travis marriage had problems, however, and within two and a half years they separated and he left for Texas.

In April 1831 he registered for land headrights and set up his law practice in Anahuac, Texas. The following year he set up a practice in San Felipe in partnership with Willie Nibbs.

Travis came into conflict twice with Mexican authorities in Anahuac: first, in 1832, when he was arrested for leading resistance against the Mexican military commandant of the town, Juan Bradburn, and again in January 1835 for leading a group which captured and disarmed a newly arrived Mexican garrison under Captain Tenorio. The incidents caused quite a disturbance among both Mexican officials and Texan settlers, who ultimately were forced to come to Travis's assistance. Travis was censured by cooler heads among the more established Texan settlers.

At the outbreak of the Texas Revolution, he was in the scouting service and then became chief of the recruiting service at San Felipe.

In November 1835 he resigned his newly appointed commission as major of artillery, requesting a position with the cavalry. On 12/24/1835 he was commissioned a lieutenant colonel of cavalry, and in January was ordered by Governor Henry Smith to reinforce Colonel Neill at Bexar. He did so reluctanly and traveled to Bexar with the company of John H. Forsyth.

Travis was unhappy with his assignment for being ordered to Bexar with so few men (only about thirty). Also, since his rank was the highest called for in the newly established Texan cavalry, he apparently felt that bigger and better assignments should have been his. Riding to the relief of a fortified position should have technically been the duty of an artillery officer.[121]

Travis arrived in Bexar, with his men, on or about 2/2/1836 and was shortly placed in command of the entire garrison when Neill left to try to obtain money for the impoverished command.

Problems with James Bowie arose over command of volunteers at the post, but these were resolved by 2/14/1836, when Travis and Bowie agreed to a joint command.

Upon the return of the Mexican forces, on 2/23/1836, Travis led his command into the Alamo. He regained full command of the garrison on the following day, when Bowie was incapacitated by illness.

His letters from the Alamo give valuable information as to the progress of the siege and the condition of the garrison. They also record his praise for the conduct of the men under fire.

On the morning of 3/6/1836, William B. Travis died at his post on the north wall of the Alamo by a single bullet wound to the head, only minutes into the Alamo battle. His death was witnessed and reported by his slave, Joe, who was by his side.

Travis is generally described as being about six feet tall, 175 pounds, sinewy and rawboned. His complexion was fair and ruddy, his auburn hair short and somewhat curly, and he was clean-shaven. He had blue-gray eyes, a broad, dimpled chin, and a high, white forehead.[122]

Travis was known for his somewhat dramatic and fiery nature, yet at times he tended to be moody. He was a man who liked to communicate. He wrote many letters and kept a diary. He enjoyed a drink now and then, gambling, flashy clothing and the company of many women. But he also had a fond weakness for children, especially his young son. Travis had a religious side as well, and at one time he recommended that Methodist missionaries immigrate to Texas.

Over the years, books and films have distorted Travis's personality and his role at the Alamo more so than that of any other defender.

TUMLINSON, GEORGE W. (1814–3/6/1836)
Age: 22 years
Born: Missouri
Residence: Gonzales, Texas
Rank: Private (artilleryman, Captain Carey's artillery company)
KIB

George W. Tumlinson was the son of James and Elizabeth Tumlinson.

He entered the Texas artillery under Almeron Dickerson on 9/20/1835. He took part in the siege and battle of Bexar, was discharged, and then reenlisted on 12/14/1835 at Bexar for six months of service as a member of Carey's company.

Sometime before the siege of the Alamo began, Tumlinson left Bexar for his home in Gonzales. He returned to the Alamo on 3/1/1836 with the relief force from Gonzales.

TYLEE, JAMES (1795–3/6/1836)
Age: 41 years
Born: New York
Residence: Texas
Rank: Private (rifleman)
KIB

James Tylee and his twenty-four-year-old wife Matilda applied for a land application in Texas in 1834.

It is uncertain as to which military unit he belonged to during the siege and battle of the Alamo.

WALKER, ASA (1813–3/6/1836)
Age: 23 years
Residence: Tennessee
Rank: Private (rifleman, Captain White's infantry company)
KIB

Asa Walker came to Texas in November 1835.

At Washington-on-the-Brazos he wrote a note to a Mr. Gant, whose gun and overcoat he appropriated on his way to Texas, explaining that "the hurry of the moment and my want of means to do better are all the excuse I have."[123]

He took part in the siege and battle of Bexar and remained in Bexar as a member of the Bexar Guards.

On the return of the garrison made by Colonel Neill when he left Bexar, Walker is listed as being "In hospital."[124]

Walker was a cousin of Alamo defender Jacob Walker.

WALKER, JACOB (May 1799–3/6/1836)
Age: 37 years
Born: Rockridge County, Tennessee
Residence: Nacogdoches, Texas
Rank: Private (artilleryman, Captain Carey's artillery
 company)
KIB

Jacob Walker was the brother of the famous mountain man Joseph R. Walker.

He married Sara Anne Vauchere in November 1827 and they had four children.

Walker took part in the siege and battle of Bexar and was issued a donation certificate for 640 acres of land for his service. He remained in Bexar as a member of Carey's artillery company.

Susannah Dickerson stated that toward the end of the Alamo battle, Walker rushed into the room she was occupying in the chapel, pursued by Mexican soldiers. The soldiers shot and bayonetted him to death as she looked on. She also recalled that during the siege, Walker would often speak to her about his children.[125]

Walker was a cousin of Alamo defender Asa Walker.

WARD, WILLIAM B. (1806–3/6/1836)
Age: 30 years
Born: Ireland
Rank: Sergeant (company NCO)
KIB

William B. Ward came to Texas from New Orleans.

It is uncertain as to which military unit he belonged to during the siege and battle of the Alamo.

During the presiege inactivity in Bexar, Ward gained a reputation for drunkenness. However, when the Mexican army appeared on 2/23/1836 and the Texans retreated into the Alamo, Ward was seen at the artillery position covering the main gate — sober, calm, and apparently the only soldier who knew what to do at the time.[126]

WARNELL, HENRY (1812–June 1836)
Age: 24 years (jockey, hunter)
Residence: Bastrop, Texas
Rank: Private (artilleryman, Captain Carey's artillery company)
Escaped from the Alamo during the battle on 3/6/1836, but died of wounds sustained two months later

Henry Warnell and Ludie Ragsdale were parents of a son, John. Henry left his home in Arkansas for Texas in November 1834, after Ludie died giving birth to their child. He left the infant under the care of friends.

In January 1835 he became a resident of Bastrop, Texas, where he lived with and worked for Edward Burleson.

He took part in the siege and battle of Bexar and remained in Bexar as a member of Carey's company.

Warnell escaped from the Alamo on the morning of 3/6/1836, but he died in Nacogdoches in June 1836 of wounds received in the battle. Some unverified accounts claim that he was wounded while leaving the Alamo as a courier for Travis on 2/28/1836.

Edward Burleson became the administrator of his estate. An administrator's claim for his military service totaled $39.59.

Warnell's son was his only heir and, in 1860, received two-thirds league and one labor of land, plus a donation grant of 640 acres.

Henry Warnell was described as "small, weighing less than 118 lbs, blue eyed, red-headed, freckled and an incessant tobacco chewer."[127]

His name is sometimes listed as "Wornell," "Warnal," or "Wurnall."

WASHINGTON, JOSEPH G. (1808–3/6/1836)
Age: 28 years
Born: Logan County, Kentucky
Rank: Private (rifleman, Captain Harrison's company, VAC)
KIB

Joseph G. Washington was the son of Andrew and Margaret Bridger Washington. He traveled to Texas with Peter J. Bailey, B. Archer M. Thomas, Daniel Cloud, and William Fontleroy.

He was sworn into the Volunteer Auxiliary Corps of Texas on 1/14/1836 in Nacogdoches before Judge Forbes. He traveled to Bexar and the Alamo as a member of Harrison's company, arriving there on or about 2/9/1836.

Washington may also have gone by the name of James Morgan.

WATERS, THOMAS (1812–3/6/1836)
Age: 24 years
Born: England
Residence: Same
Rank: Private (artilleryman, Captain Carey's artillery company)
KIB

Thomas Waters came to Texas by way of New Orleans as a member of Breece's New Orleans Greys.

He took part in the siege and battle of Bexar and remained in Bexar as a member of Carey's artillery company.

WELLS, WILLIAM (8/16/1798–3/6/1836)
Age: 37 years
Born: Hall County, Georgia
Residence: Same
Rank: Private (rifleman)
KIB

William Wells was the son of Charles and Sarah Lewis Wells. He was the father of a son and daughter.

He may have come to Bexar and the Alamo as a member of Captain Patton's company. Dr. John Sutherland, also a member of Patton's company, knew William well enough to advance him $20 to pay for a Yeager rifle.

WHITE, ISAAC (?–3/6/1836)
Residence: Alabama or Kentucky
Rank: Sergeant (company NCO)
KIB

Isaac White was a married man with one daughter.

It is unknown which military unit he served with during the siege and battle of the Alamo.

WHITE, ROBERT (1806–3/6/1836)
Age: 30 years
Residence: Gonzales, Texas
Rank: Captain (commanding officer of infantry company)
KIB

Robert White took part in the siege and battle of Bexar as a lieutenant. He remained in Bexar and was promoted to captain by 2/4/1836. He took command of one of the garrison's infantry companies, the Bexar Guards.

It is possible that White left Bexar sometime before the siege of the Alamo began, returned to his home in Gonzales, and came back to the Alamo with the relief force from Gonzales.

WILLIAMSON, HIRAM JAMES (1810–3/6/1836)
Age: 26 years
Born: Philadelphia, Pennsylvania
Residence: Washington-on-the-Brazos, Texas
Rank: Sergeant major (ranking NCO of the Alamo garrison staff)
KIB

Hiram J. Williamson was the son of Hiram Williamson, Sr.

In 1835 he was an unsuccessful candidate for the office of *alcalde* of Washington-on-the-Brazos.

He took part in the siege and battle of Bexar and remained in Bexar as the sergeant major of the garrison. As such, he was the highest ranking enlisted man at the Alamo.

The administrator of his estate was Thomas S. Saul.

Williamson's name is sometimes listed as "H. S. Williamson."

WILLS, WILLIAM (?–3/6/1836)
Farmer
Residence: Brazoria County, Texas
Rank: Private (rifleman)
KIB

Very little is known about William Wills. The only record of his role at the Alamo is a will probated in Brazoria County, Texas, in May 1836, stating that he died at the Alamo.

WILSON, DAVID L. (1807–3/6/1836)
Age: 29 years
Born: Scotland
Residence: Nacogdoches, Texas
Rank: Private (rifleman, possibly Captain Dimitt's company)
KIB

David L. Wilson was the son of James and Susanna Wesley Wilson. His wife, Ophelia, was the administrator of his estate. Ophelia later married Albert Henning.

David may have been one of the volunteers who accompanied Philip Dimitt to Bexar and the Alamo.

WILSON, JOHN (1804–3/6/1836)
Age: 32 years
Born: Pennsylvania
Rank: Private (rifleman)
KIB

John Wilson was the son of John and Jane Nevin Wilson.

There were at least six John Wilsons in the Texan army during the Texas Revolution.

Little is known about this defender, other than his death at the Alamo.

WOLF, ANTHONY (2/17/1782–3/6/1836)
Age: 54 years (Served as a Lieutenant of Infantry in the
  Louisiana Territorial Militia in 1806.)
Residence: Washington County, Texas
Rank: Private (artilleryman, Captain Carey's artillery
  company)
KIB

Anthony Wolf lived in the Louisiana-Texas territory before 1820.

On 9/15/1818 he was sent as an emissary to the Wichita Indians on the Brazos River, the first individual who would agree to do so. He returned to Natchitoches, Louisiana, in mid-January of 1819.[128]

On 10/6/1822, Wolf relocated to Nacogdoches, Texas, and was introduced to Governor Tres Palacios by James Dill, who described Wolf as having been "[b]orn and raised a Spanish subject . . ." In Texas, Wolf continued to serve as an Indian agent and on 11/8/1822 was a member of an expedition to treat with the Cherokee Indians.[129]

Sometime prior to the Texas Revolution, Wolf went through a long illness. He convalesced in the home of John W. Hall at Washington-on-the-Brazos.[130]

Following the siege and battle of Bexar, he served as a member of Captain Carey's artillery company.[131] He died in the battle of the Alamo on 3/6/1836.

In 1878 an Ohio journalist, Charles W. Evers, interviewed Susannah Hannig (nee Dickerson). Evers wrote, "She says that only one man, named Wolff, asked for quarter, but was instantly killed. The wretched man had two little boys, aged 11 and 12 years. The little fellows came to Mrs. Dickerson's room, where the Mexicans killed them and a man named Walker, and carried the boys bodies out on their bayonets."[132]

In 1841 Mary V. Tauzin (nee Durst), claiming to be

Wolf's widow, filed for one league and labor of land due him for his service. The rear of the form is marked "Dec. 14 . . . Public Lands . . . unfavorable," indicating that she probably did not receive the claim.[133]

Anthony Wolf is listed as the third husband of Mary V. Durst in the Durst family genealogy. Why she did not receive the land is unknown. The genealogy also lists them as having had a son, although it does not give a name.[134]

Also in 1841, an attorney, David S. Kaufman, was named as the administrator of Wolf's estate.[135]

His name has been given as "Wolfe," "Woolf," and "Wollf."

WOLF CHILDREN
Ages: 11 and 12 years
Rank: Noncombatants
KIB

According to Susannah (Dickerson) Hannig, two unarmed children were brutally bayonetted by Mexican troops during the battle. She identified them as the children of one of the Alamo's gunners named "Wolff."[136]

Why these children were in the Alamo with their father is unknown, as is the identity of their mother.

WRIGHT, CLAIBORNE (1810–3/6/1836)
Age: 26 years
Born: North Carolina
Residence: Gonzales, Texas
Rank: Private (rifleman, Gonzales Ranging Company)
KIB

Claiborne Wright was the son of James and Patsy Stigall Wright.

He entered the Texan army on 11/10/1835 and took part in the siege and battle of Bexar. He was discharged on 12/13/1835 and returned to his home in Gonzales.

He returned to the Alamo as a member of the relief force from Gonzales, arriving there on 3/1/1836.

XIMENES, DAMACIO (?–3/6/1836)
Born: Probably Texas
Residence: Texas
Rank: Private (rifleman)
KIB

Damacio Ximenes was a widower and had one son who died in childhood.

He took part in the actions at Anahuac in 1835 and in the siege and battle of Bexar.

He was one of the soldiers who helped transport the eighteen-pound cannon, which was of great use during the taking of Bexar and later was the Alamo's largest artillery piece.

After the Alamo battle, his body was identified by Cornelio Delgado, who was one of the party in charge of disposing of the dead.

His heirs were his nephew and niece, Juan and Gertrudis Ximenes, who filed claims in 1861.

Damacio Ximenes has only recently been recognized as a defender of the Alamo.

ZANCO, CHARLES (1808–3/6/1836)
Age: 28 years (painter, farmer)
Born: Randers, Denmark
Residence: Harris County, Texas
Rank: Lieutenant (assistant to ordnance chief, Ordnance Dept.)
KIB

Charles Zanco was the son of Frederick Zanco of Denmark, and a single man. He and his father immigrated to America in 1834 after the death of Charles's mother. They settled in Harris County, Texas.

At the outbreak of the Texas Revolution, Zanco joined a company called the "First Volunteers at Lynchburg," in the autumn of 1835. When the company devised a flag, it became Zanco's duty to paint the chosen design on it. The design was a single star with the word "Independence," so Zanco may hold the distinction of being the first person to paint a "Lone Star" on a Texas flag.

He took part in the siege and battle of Bexar as a member of the artillery service. According to Colonel Neill, Zanco "discharged his duty as such in a faithful manner."[137]

After the battle, Charles Zanco remained in Bexar. He was promoted to lieutenant and served as an assistant to the ordnance chief, Robert Evans. As such, he would have been responsible for the maintenance and care of the garrison's firearms and munitions.

Zanco was the only native of Denmark to die at the Alamo. His father was his only heir and was living in St. Louis, Missouri, in 1852.

His name is often listed incorrectly on Texan records as "Zanor," "Lance," and "Danor."

Part II

Their Words

"In their own way, the ghosts speak."
— Mardell Plainfeather [1]

"I start for Antonio in the morning and hope to be there by the time the battering cannon arrive from New Orleans. We want all the guns, ammunition and men you can send. The Volunteers are received with open arms by the people, and, as you see by the proceedings of the Convention, are properly announced. The Americans are within four hundred yards of San Antonio and waiting until cannon, &c. shall be received. The Texians, as you will see, have made a Declaration of Independence — it amounts to a Declaration, although not worded in the same manner as old Tom Jefferson's. The State of Mississippi must send forth her gallant sons to aid us. Many have come — God bless them — like brave descendents of worthy sire. — They must not let Louisiana bear away the palm. We look to Mississippi particularly for aid in this crisis; she stands high in the estimation of the people of Texas for patriotism and liberality, and do not let her fall below the mark, if your exertions can prevent it."

CHARLES A. PARKER
Nacogdoches, Texas
11/20/1835[2]

128

"I have left my own dear, native land, my relations and friends, the companions of my early years, and every thing that I held dear and valuable, with a view to come to Texas to seek an establishment and home for myself; . . . I feel a great desire to render some service to this country of my adoption in her struggle for freedom, and would be happy if I could go in the field in any other attitude than a common soldier."

JOHN C. GOODRICH
Washington, Texas
11/28/1835[3]

"Permit me, through you to volunteer my services in the present struggle of Texas without conditions. I shall receive nothing, either in the form of service pay, or lands or rations."

JAMES B. BONHAM
San Felipe, Texas
12/1/1835[4]

"I have taken passage in the steamboat Pacific and shall leave in an hour or two . . . I have met in the same boat a number of acquaintances from Nashville and the District, bound for Texas, among whom are George C. Childress and his brother. Childress thinks the fighting will be over before we get there, and speaks cheeringly of the prospects. I feel more energy than I ever did in anything I have undertaken. I am determined to provide for you a home or perish . . . Fare you all well till you hear from me again, perhaps from Natchez."

MICAJAH AUTRY
Memphis, Tennessee
12/7/1835[5]

"We, the undersigned have embarked on board the Schooner Santiago, on the 9th December, 1835, at New Orleans, for Texas, to relieve our oppressed brethren who have emigrated thither by inducements held forth to them by the Mexican government, and rights guaranteed to settlers of that province, which that government now denies them; and in our opinion, their situation is assimilated to that of our forefathers, who labored under tyrannical oppression.

". . . We hereby declare that we have left every endearment at our respective places of abode in the United States of America, to maintain and defend our brethren, at the peril of our lives, liberties and fortunes."

RICHARD W. BALLENTINE
CLEVELAND K. SIMMONS et al.
On board the *Santiago*
12/9/1835[6]

"About 20 minutes ago I landed at this place safely after considerable peril . . . The war is still going on favourably to the Texans, but it is thought that Santa Anna will make a descent with his whole forces in the Spring, but there will be soldiers enough of the real grit in Texas by that time to overrun all Mexico.

". . . We have between 400 and 500 miles to foot it to the seat of government, for we cannot get horses, but we have sworn allegiance to each other and will get along somehow . . . The smallpox has recently broken out here very bad, but I fear the Tavern bill a great deal worse. Such charges were never heard of and we have to stay here probably several days before we can procure a conveyance for our baggage. I suppose we shall join and buy a waggon.

". . . Write me in Texas by every private opportunity, and I will do the same."

MICAJAH AUTRY
Natchitoches, Louisiana
12/13/1835[7]

"I submit to you letters of introduction and recommendation from my friends in Louisville, which I would have been proud to have handed you in person, but circumstances being such as to compel me to forward them by some other conveyance. I have only to signify that I wish to be attached to your regular army which is now organizing. As will be seen by the letters aforesaid, I am a volunteer from Kentucky and have come to Texas to aid in her struggle; and if it would meet your approbation, I would be proud to hold a station among the officers of her army.

"The company to which I belong have conferred upon me the rank of first Lieutenant. I wish to remain in the cause of Texas until the termination of her struggle, and any post which you in your friendship and liberality may confer. I promise you shall be maintained with honor and dignity by your humble servant . . .

"We will depart for St. Antonio in tomorrow."

JOHN M. THURSTON
Washington, Texas
12/18/1835[8]

"A long time has elapsed since we parted and long before this period, I expected to write to you, but continual traveling and employment have prevented. After leaving Uncle Sloan's in Missouri which we did on the 29th of November, we journeyed South. I left the family well except Grandma, who was extremely ill. I have no idea that she yet lives. I left upwards of $30.00 with her besides the $10.00 sent her by Uncle William, which made between forty and fifty dollars, which I deem sufficient in the event of life or death . . .

"Now you wish me to say something of the country through which we have traveled, Viz, Illinois, Missouri, Arkansas and Louisiana . . .

"The soil of Ill. North of 38 degrees is the best I ever saw and from all I can learn, the best body of land on earth of the same extent . . .

"The reasons which induced us to travel on were briefly these, First our curiosity was unsatisfied, second, Law Dockets were not large, fees low, and yankee lawyers numerous, Third the coldness of the Climate . . .

"Our reason for not stopping in Mo. were first we were disappointed in the face of the country and the coldness of the climate, but most of all the smallness of the docket. There is less litigation in this State than in any other State in the Union, . . . and what is going on rebounds very little to the emolument of the practitioner . . .

"We found Ark. Territory, in some places rich, well

watered, and healthy and society tolerably good, but the great body of the country is stoney sandy and mountainous . . . Had we chosen to locate in Ark. we would have made money rapidly, if blessed with health and life. Dockets and funds being large. The reason for our pushing still further on must now be told and as it is a Master one, it will suffice without the mention of any other. Ever since Texas has unfurled the banner of freedom, and commenced a warfare for liberty or death, our hearts have been enlisted in her behalf. The progress of her cause has increased the ardor of our feelings until we have resolved to embark in the vessel which contains the flag of Liberty and sink or swim in it's defense . . .

"The cause of Philanthropy, of Humanity, of Liberty and human happiness throughout the world, called loudly on every man who can to aid Texas . . .

"If we succeed, the Country is ours. It is immense in extent, and fertile in its soil, and will amply reward all our toil. If we fail, death in the cause of liberty and humanity is not cause for shuddering . . .

"I hope I shall recover entirely the hardships I am destined to undergo. Mr. Bailey has fine health, we have been traveling ten weeks, and have gone over about twenty five hundred miles.

"If I were with you, I could talk enough to tire you. I hope we shall meet."

DANIEL W. CLOUD
Near Natchitoches, Louisiana
12/26/1835[9]

"We have found many situations suitable for the profitable employment of legal qualifications, but our hopes, our feelings, and sympatheties urged us on, and now we stand on the shores of the United States, but next week, heaven willing, we shall breathe the air of Texas. Nor do we go to Texas as mere spectators of the momentous transactions now going on in that fertile region; no, we go with arms in our hands, determined to conquer or die; resolved to bury our all in the same ditch which ingulphs the liberties of Texas, or see it freed from this Government . . .

132

". . . Mexico can no more conquer Texas than she can Louisiana — She may occupy the extent of soil her soldiery encamp upon — but no more. Texas can battle it for years. Yet we do wish to see an end put to the further effusion of blood . . .

"If we succeed, a fertile region and a grateful people will be for us our home and secure to us our reward. If we fail, death in defense of so just and so good a cause need not exclte a shudder or a tear.

"Thousands of magnanimous youths from all quarters of this mighty nursery of freemen are pushing on to the seat of war, and many are destined to signalize themselves and win renown in the war of Texas.

"When Texas becomes free I see in prospective a charming picture . . . opulence, security, intelligence, religious and moral excellence, and social happiness and refinement . . . The prospect is grand, too much so for my feeble power of description to compass."

DANIEL W. CLOUD
Natchitoches, Louisiana
Late December 1835[10]

"My dear son and daughter: this is the first time I have to write to you with convenience. I am now blessed with excellent health, and am in high spirits, although I have had many difficulties to encounter. I have got through safe and have been received by everybody with open arms of friendship, I am hailed with a hearty welcome to this country, a dinner and a party of Ladys have honored me with an invitation to participate with them, both in Nacogdoches and this place; the cannon was fired here on my arrival and I must say as to What I have seen of Texas, it is the garden spot of the world, the best land & best prospects for health I ever saw is here; there is a world of country to settle, it is not required to pay down for your league of land; everyman is entitled to his headright of 4438 A. and they make the money to pay for it off the land.

"I expect in all probability to settle on the Bodark or Chocktaw Bayou of Red River, that I have no doubt is the richest country in the world, good land, plenty of timber, and the best springs, and good mill streams, good range, clear water & every appearance of health — game a plenty. It is in the pass where the buffalo passes from the north to south and back twice a year and bees and honey a plenty.

"I have great hope of getting the agency to settle that country and I would be glad to see every friend I have settle there, it would be a fortune to them all. I have taken the oath of the government and have enrolled my name as a volunteer for six months, and will set out for the Rio Grande in a few days with the volunteers of the U.S., but all volunteers are entitled to a vote for a member of the convention and these members are to be voted for; and I have but little doubt of being elected a member to form the Constitution for the Provence. I am rejoiced at my fate. I had rather be in my present situation than to be elected to a seat in Congress for life. I am in great hopes of making a fortune for myself and family bad as has been my prospects. I have not wrote to William but have requested John to direct him what to do. I hope you show him this letter and also your brother John as it is not convenient at this time for me to write them. I hope you will do the best you can and I will do the same, do not be uneasy about me I am with my friends. I must close with great respects

Your affectionate father, Farewell."

DAVID CROCKETT
San Augustine, Texas
1/9/1836[11]

"I arrived at Washington on the 28th of July. This is a small town situated on the Brazos river & there I intended to take up my final residence, but the unsettled state of affairs between Texas & the Mexican Government, I was called to the field . . . This place [Bexar] is an ancient Mexican fort & Town divided by a small river which eminates from Springs. The town has two Squares in and the church in the centre, one a military and the other a government square. The Alamo or the fort as we call it, is a very old building, built for the purpose of protecting the citizens from hostile Indians. The Mexican army or rather part of them came to this place commanded by Martin de Perfecto de Coss . . . The enemy (as I

134

shall now call them) sent about 200 of their troops to Gonzales after a cannon that they sent there for the use of the citizens to fight the indians . . . Volunteers was called for to fight for their country I was one of the first that started, about 150 of us ready in a moments warning, and we marched to Gonzales and put the enemy to flight they retreated to this place, . . . they commenced fortifying the town and strengthening the alamo until it became almost impossible to overcome them, our number increased gradually to the amount of 800 but on account of so many office seekers there was nothing but confusion, contention and discord throughout the encampment, . . . We rallied around a brave soul (Colo Milam) and requested him to be our leader, he consented and 150 of us declared to take the place or die in the attempt, while a large number of them endeavored to discourage us and said we would all be butchered, but a few more seen we were resolute and joined untill our number was 220, and on the next morning about day break we marched in the town under heavy fires of their cannon & musketry, but we succeeded in getting possession of some stone houses (which is outside the square) that sheltered us a little from their fires until we could make Breastworks for ourselves we labored hard day and night for five days still gaining possession when on the morning of the 5th day they sent in a flag of truce to the extreme joy of us all, . . . on the third day of the siege our leader fell in the battle, another userped his command who never was in favor of storming . . . but he was in time to make a disgraceful treaty, some strongly suspect bribery was the cause but whether or ignorance I cannot decide . . . We should have made a Treaty and not a childs bargain however its done now and its too late to alter until we have another fight which we expect shortly.

"... I volunteered as a private and as a private in camp was always ready and willing to discharge the duty of a soldier when called on. I was out on a number of scouts and would frequently creep up to the Mexican sentinals at a late hour when they thought alls well and shoot one or two of them of a night — and Oh! my dear sister and brothers how often have I thought of you when I have been walking the lonely wood or barren fields as a sentinel exposed to all the inclemencies of

135

the weather and suffering many privations which you can not have the least idea of. but all was sweet when I reflected on our forefathers in the strugle of liberty. about the 28th of October I was appointed 2d Lieut. of artillery and during the siege I was promoted to first on account of the first Lieut. being cashiered for cowardice he always use the word go and I come on my brave boys. I thought & still think that nothing but fate save me we only had four killed and thirteen wounded three of the wounded & two of the killed received the shots along side of me when discharging their duty at a cannon that was ordered by a fool in the open street immediately before the enemies breastworks within 120 yards of their heavy fires, but he was my Superior and I did obey and when the men was killed & wounded I loaded and fired the gun assisted by two more instead of ten and escaped only slightly wounded, a ball passed through my hat and cut the flesh to the scull bone and my clothes received many shots until a lucky shot made by me into the porthole of the Enemy I dismounted their cannon which caused them to cease firing untill we got our away . . . the wound never prevented me from working the guns. After we took the place . . . volunteers was called for to inlist for four months . . . they were to form into companies and elect their officers — fifty six brave souls joined into a company of artillery and chose me for their Captain. I accepted the command and my dear sister is it possible that the once ignorant weak and fickle minded W. R. Carey should now be at the head of so many brave men as their leader . . . The forces here is commanded by Lieut. Colo J. C. Neill who has his quarters in the Town which is called the left wing of the forces and your brother William has the command of the alamo which is called the right wing I am subject to the orders of Colo Neill but he thinks a great deal of my judgement and consults me about a number of proceedings before he issues an order. Brothers and sister do not think that I am vain my friends here says I don't possess enough vanity for my own good, except when we go to fight the Enemy and then I think a small number of us can whip an army of Mexicans — I know one thing, I am deceived in myself.

"When I was in Natchitoches I wrote to you and stated I

believe that soon I should look out for a companion. It would have happened this winter if the war had not commenced but fortunately it did. My selection was nothing to boast of she is tolerably ugly and tolerably poor and tolerably illiterate, but she is virtuous and a good hosekeeper, but there is no prospect now, as I was conversing with a Mexican lady the other day she remarked that in time of peace the ladies would gladly embrace the offer or accept the hand of an officer, but in these war times they would too soon become a widow. She may be right but I don't think it, however I have too much else to think about now. As I have not been a graduate at West point, I must study military affairs now for I am rejoiced at the oportunity to do something for myself. The men in this place have sometimes been discouraged on account of the distressed situation we are in; for want of clothes and food. The Colo and myself has twice called a general parade and addressed them in such a manner that they would get satisfied for awhile, but we are now discouraged ourselves, and unless the provisional government of Texas do speedily send us assistance we will abandon the place, we have sent and made known our situation to them, and as the safety of Texas depends mostly upon the keeping of this place they certainly will as soon as possible do some thing for us especially when we expect to declare independence as soon as the convention meets . . .

"I cannot close without saying something about my invincibles, as I call them, about twenty of my company (although the whole has been tried and I know them all) that will (to use their words) wade through h-ll, when I am at their head if I should give the order — O sister could you but see me at the head of these brave men marching forward (undismayed) to perform their duty. To relate circumstances of their bravery it would fill a large book. When the enemy ten to one has marched up as if they in one minute would send us all to eternity to see the invincibles rush forward charge upon them and put them to flight except those we would either kill or take prisoners. We have had many such scirmishes since we left home. A circumstance occurred the other day which I must relate, a man for disobedience of orders and bad conduct was ordered to arrested (he was not under my command) The

officer who received this order took a file of men and attempted to arrest him — he resisted and swore with pistols in
his hands that he would shoot down the first man that attempted his arrest, the officer retreated without him the Colo
immediately sent an order to me informing me of the circumstance and requesting me to take a file of my invincibles and
bring the culprit to. I ordered three of the brave to prepare immediately I buckled on my sword and went to him he was
then with two more who also swore he should not be taken. I
approached him with my men he told me if I came one step
further he would certainly shoot me down the other two swore
the same and with great confidence too as he had put the
other off but he soon found himself mistaken my men wanted
to rush immediately upon them I ordered them to halt and I
walked up to him and with a mild tone told him to disarm
himself or I would cut him assunder he sheepishly laid down
his pistols and gave himself up, the other two swore still that
we should not take him. I insignificantly look up and told
them if they attempted to move or put their finger on the trig-
ger of their arms that they should fall on the spot they stood. I
then walked up to them and took their arms likewise, . . .
When any thing of a dangerous character is to be done its by
order Capt Carey will take a file from comp. of his men and go
immediately and ———. It's always done . . . I must close by
saying that if I live, as soon as the war is over I will endeavor
to see you all."

WILLIAM R. CAREY
San Antonio de Bexar
1/12/1836[12]

"I have reached this point after many hardships and privations but thank God in most excellent health. The very
great fatigue I have suffered has in a degree stifled reflection
and has been an advantage to me . . . Capt. Kimble from
Clarksville, Ten. a lawyer of whom you may recollect to have
heard me speak arrived with a small company of select men, 4
of them lawyers. I joined them and find them perfect gentlemen . . . we shall join Houston the commander in chief and receive our destination. I may or may not receive promotion as

there are many very meritorious men seeking the same. I have become one of the most thorough going men you ever heard of. I go the whole Hog in the cause of Texas. I expect to help them gain their independence and also to form their civil government, for it is worth risking many lives for. From what I have seen and learned from others there is not so fair a portion of the earth's surface warmed by the sun.

"Be of good cheer Martha I will provide you a sweet home. I shall be entitled to 640 acres of land for my services in the army and 4444 acres upon condition of settling my family here. Whether I shall be able to move you here next fall or not will depend upon the termination of the present contest. Some say that Santa Ana is in the field with an immense army and near the confines of Texas, others say that since the conquest of St. Antonio by the Texians and the imprisonment of Genl. Cos and 1100 men of which you have no doubt heard, that Santa Ana has become intimidated for fear that the Texians will drive the war into his dominions and is now holding himself in readiness to fly to Europe which latter report I am inclined to discredit, what is the truth of the matter no one here knows or pretends to know.

". . . Give my most kind affection to Amelia and Mr. Smith and to my own Dear Mary and James give a thousand tender embraces and for you my Dearest Martha may the smile of heaven keep you as happy as possible till we meet . . .

"p.s. We stand guard of nights and night before last was mine to stand two hours during which the moon rose in all her mildness but splendor and majesty. With what pleasure did I contemplate that lovely orb chiefly because I recollected how often you and I have taken pleasure in standing in the door and contemplating her together. Indeed I imagined that you might be looking at her at the same time. Farewell Dear Martha.

"p.s. Col. Crockett has just joined our company."

MICAJAH AUTRY
Nacogdoches, Texas
1/13/1836[13]

"From the necessity of the case, I have been compelled to use all my private stock of money which I intended for my

139

own individual expenses in order to promote & cherish the enlistment of Soldiers in the Legion of Cavalry in the payment of small Bills at boarding houses, Taverns & the like & believing I cannot be servisable without money, I would therefore solicit your hon. body if possibly within its power to allow me to draw on the treasurer for fifty dollars to be paid out of the contingent fund as an advance of my future pay for which sum I will account."

JOHN H. FORSYTH
San Felipe, Texas
1/13/1836[14]

"I have but a moment to write you as I am so busy regulating the Hospital — Things have been in the worst possible state here as you are aware — I hope and have reason to believe they will soon become much better — I ought to have written by the express but knew not when it started — I have only collected on goods that are being brought into this place and the Commandant will do it, yet he is ignorant of the rate of duties established by the government — Were he in possession of that knowledge he would avail himself of it now as there are goods here and he talks of charging but four per cent — I am interested in this you will see for the Hospital is in great want of a little money — We shall endeavor to elect as many of our countrymen as possible from this jurisdiction — what the prospect is I have not yet been able to learn — I think we have now an excellent opportunity to completely conquer our most formidable foe our internal enemy — the Mexican tory party of the country — I hope every friend of his country will be dilligent at his post and from the righteousness of our cause we cannot but succeed."

AMOS POLLARD
San Antonio de Bexar
1/16/1836[15]

"Believing that a letter will meet you at Goliad, and having had more time to make a better plot of the 'Fortress Alamo' at this place have embraced this conveyance, to acquaint you more satisfactorily of the condition and progress of the department, which you have so kindly assigned me.

"I send you herewith inclosed a neat plot of the fortress . . . showing the improvements already made by me.

"I am now fortifying and mounting the cannon. The 18 pounder now on the N.W.[16] corner of the fortress so as to command the Town and the country around.

"The officers of every department do more work than the men and also stand guard, and act as patrol every night. I have no doubt but the enemy have spies in town every twenty-four hours, and we are using our utmost endeavors to catch them every night, nor have I any doubt but there are 1500 of the enemy at the town of Rio Grande, and as many more at Laredo, and I believe they know our situation as well as we do ourselves.

"We have received 100 bushels of meal and 42 Beeves which will last us for two months yet to come, but no other supplies have come to our relief . . .

"We can rely on aid from the citizens of this town in case of a siege, Saquine [Seguin] is doing all for the cause he can, as well as many of the most wealthy and influential citizens.

"You can plainly see by the plot that the Alamo never was built by a military people for a fortress, tho' it is strong, there is not a redoubt that will command the whole line of the fort, all is in the plain wall and intended to take advantage with a few piece of artillery, it is a strong place and better that it should remain as it is after completing the half moon batteries than to rebuild it. The men here will not labour and I cannot ask it of them untill they are better clad and fed. We now have 114 men counting officers, the sick and wounded which leaves us about 80 efficient men. 40 in the Alamo and 40 in Town, leaving all of the patrole duty to be done by the officers and which for want of horses has to be performed on foot.

"We have had loose discipline untill lately. Since we heard of 1000 to 1500 men of the enemy being on their march to this place duty is being done well and punctually in case of an attack we will move all into the Alamo and whip 10 to 1 with our artillery.

"If the men here can get a reasonable supply of clothing, provisions and money they will remain the balance of the 4 months and do duty and fight better than fresh men, they have all been tried and have confidence in themselves . . .

"I have been much flattered for my exertions at this place. I have more than one time received the vote of thanks of the whole Garrison . . .

"I will in my next give you a plan of the Town as fortified when we took it. We have too few to garrison both places, and will bring all our forces to the Alamo tomorrow as well as the cannons."

GREEN B. JAMESON
San Antonio de Bexar
1/18/1836[17]

"The scarcity of paper together with other difficulties I have had to labour under has prevented me from writing before this and indeed it is a matter of Claim whether this letter will ever reach the United States.

"I arrived at the mouth of the Brazos about a month ago in a vessel from New Orleans and have traveled on foot by San Felipe to this place leaving my trunk with book, and two rifles with Mr. White at Columbia 10 miles above Brazoria having sold my best rifle for $30 at San Felipe. I saw Genl. Houston and Presented him your letter. He advised me to get a horse & proceed to Goliad where he would see me in a short time again — I have accordingly come on thus far with that intention as to connect myself with a Company of Rangers on the Frontiers to keep off the Indians, But it is most probable I will go on to San Antonio de Bexar until I can suitably connect myself with the Army or until an occasion may require my services. Every man in this country at this time has to go upon his own footing as the Government at present is unable to make any provisions for the Army. However a change for the better is expected soon and affairs is expected to be in a better condition . . .

"Tho under rather different circumstances myself at this time, I have no reason to complain of my coming to this country as I find nothing but what might have been expected. On the contrary I have the satisfaction of beholding one of the finest countries in the world and have fully determined to locate myself in Texas I hope to be better situated to write you more about this country . . .

"Letters have been intercepted to the Mexican citizens of

Bexar informing them of the arrival of 2,000 troops on the Rio Grande, and now coming on to retake that place in consequence of which, Many of the Mexicans have secretly left the place, and preparations are now making to fortify the town."

DAVID P. CUMMINGS
Gonzales, Texas
1/20/1836[18]

"While I am waiting to carry an express to Gen. Houston, I take the opportunity of giving you my sentiments by our express to San Felipe.

"By the documents you will receive you will perceive our indignation at this post at the disorderly and anarchical conduct of the council. Were it not for a proclamation issued from headquarters which arrived here last night, you would have MEN, not SENTIMENT at San Felipe to sustain you in the discharge of your duty as first Magistrate of the nation. Be consoled! Fight the good fight and we are with you to a man. Let the low, intriguing land and Mexican speculators know, that the sons of Washington and St. Patrick will not submit to delusion, rascality and usurpation. We are bound to you in the proper discharge of your duties and will not submit to anarchy and misrule. May God bless you and prosper you is the sincere wish of an honest son of Erin and a friend to Texian Independence."

JOSEPH M. HAWKINS
San Antonio de Bexar, Texas
1/20/1836[19]

"I have this day sent you orders about contracting with McKinny for our uniforms and equipment. I wish you to attend to it immediately. I spoke to him about my uniform, which I have written to him to purchase. I am ordered off to the defense of San Antonio, which is threatened with an attack from the enemy. I shall leave in two days. Do all you can to make recruits and get the remain."

WILLIAM B. TRAVIS
San Felipe, Texas
1/21/1836[20]

143

"You will perceive by the express which leaves here today, that we may in a short time expect stormy gales from Mexico; That Santa Anna has proscribed every individual, without distinction of age or sex, from the Grande to the Sabine. He will be warmly received and nobly encountered, and find that to conquer Mexicans is one thing, but Americans another, if the latter will only do their duty by preparing with energy . . . Let a copy of the express of today be published, and circulated as far as practicable throughout the United States and Sta. Anna will boast no more, America will be triumphant, and Texas free . . .

". . . Every man here is for Independence."

JOSEPH M. HAWKINS
San Antonio de Bexar
1/24/1836[21]

"I perceive that the tory party have bought up your council and instead of being an assistant to you as intended they have usurped the government to themselves, — but the people will not stand this — you will see by our resolutions here that we are determined to support you at all hazards. — I did hope that the provisional government would continue till we could establish another and more firm one — This we shall endeavor to do in March and God grant that we may create an independent government — Should we be previously invaded I hope that the council will come back from its corrupt course and meet the exigencies of the country — Reports say that troops are now on their way. — Rely my Dear Sir on every support that my feeble efforts can give you in endeavoring to ensure the liberties and establish the Independence of our adopted country."

AMOS POLLARD
San Antonio de Bexar
1/27/1836[22]

"In obedience to my orders, I have done everything in my power to get ready to march to the relief of Bexar, but owing to the difficulty of getting horses and provisions, and owing to desertions, I shall march to-day with only about thirty men, all regulars except four. I shall, however, go on and do my duty, if I am sacrificed, unless I receive new orders to countermarch. Our affairs are gloomy indeed — the people are cold & indifferent — they are wore down by & exhausted with the war, & in consequence of dissentions between contending & rival chieftans, they have lost all confidence in their own govt. & officers. You have no idea of exhausted state of the country — volunteers can no longer be had or relied upon — A speedy organization, classification & draft of the Militia is all that can save us now. A regular army is necessary — but money, & money only can raise & equip a regular army — Money must be raised or Texas is gone to ruin — without it war cannot be again carried on in Texas — The patriotism of a few has done much; but that is becoming worn down — I have strained every nerve — I have used my personal credit & have neither slept day or night since I received orders to march — and with all this exertion, I have barely been able to get horses and equipment for the few men I have — Enclosed I send you a list of men who deserted on the road from Washington & San Felipe to this place.

"I understand . . . that His Excellency the Commandant General Sam Houston is gone to San Felipe — will you be good enough to show this communication to him & request him to write me — as I wish to be in communication with him."

WILLIAM B. TRAVIS
Burnham's, Colorado River, Texas
1/28/1836[23]

"This will be handed to you by Capt. Jackson, who will explain to you the situation of things here — I leave here with the troops under Capt. Forsyth, but shall await your orders at Gonzales or some other point on the road — I shall however keep the 30 men of Forsyth's Company in motion towards Bexar, so that they may arrive there as soon as possible —

"Not having been able to raise 100 volunteers agreeably to your order, & there being so few regular troops together, I must beg that your Excellency will recall the order for me to go on to Bexar in command of so few men — I am willing, nay anxious to go to the defense of Bexar, and I have done every-

thing in my power to equip the enlisted men & get them off —
But sir, I am unwilling to risk my reputation (which is ever
dear to a soldier) by going off into the enemies' country with
such little means, so few men, & them so badly equipted — In
fact there is no necessity for my services to command these few
men — The company officers will be amply sufficient — They
should at all events be sent to Bexar or the frontier of Nueces
— They may now go on to San Antonio under command of
Capt. Forsyth where they can be employed if necessary, if they
are not needed there they may be sent to San Patricio or some
other point — I am now convinced that none but defensive
measures can be pursued at this inclement season — If the Executive or the Major Genl. desire or order it, I will visit the
Post of San Antonio or any other for the purpose of consulting
or communicating with the officers in command there — or to
execute any commission I may be entrusted with, but I do not
feel disposed to go to command a squad of men, & without the
means of carrying on a campaign — Therefore I hope your
Excellency will take my situation into consideration, or relieve
me from the orders which I have heretofore received, so far as
they compel me to command in person the men who are now
on their way to Bexar — Otherwise I shall feel it due to myself
to resign my commission. I would remark that I can be more
useful at present, in superintending the recruiting service."

WILLIAM B. TRAVIS
Burnham's, Colorado River, Texas
1/29/1836[24]

"In pursuance of your orders, I proceeded from San Felipe to La Bahia [Goliad] and whilst there employed my
whole time trying to effect the objects of my mission . . .
Whilst at La Bahia Genl Houston received despatches from
Col Comdt. Neill informing that good reasons were enter-
tained that an attack would soon be made by a numerous
Mexican Army on our important post of Bejar. I was forth-
with determined that I should go instantly to Bejar; accordingly I left Genl Houston and with a few very efficient volunteers came on to this place about 2 weeks since. I was received
by Col Neill with great cordiality, and the men under my com-

mand entered at once into active service. All I can say of the
soldiers stationed here is complimentary to both their courage
and their patience. But it is the truth and your Excellency
must know it, that great and just dissatisfaction is felt for want
of a little money to pay the small but necessary expenses of our
men. I cannot eulogise the conduct & character of Col Neill
too highly: no other man in the army could have kept men at
this post, under the neglect they have experienced. Both he &
myself have done all that we could; we have industriously
tryed all expedients to raise funds; but hitherto it has been to
no purpose. We are still labouring night and day, laying up
provisions for a siege, encouraging our men, and calling on the
Government for relief.

"Relief at this post, in men, money & provisions is of vital
importance & is wanted instantly . . . The salvation of Texas
depends in great measure in keeping Bejar out of the hands of
the enemy. It serves as the frontier picquet guard and if it
were in the possession of Santa Anna there is no strong hold
from which to repell him in his march towards the Sabine.
There is no doubt that very large forces are being gathered in
several of the towns beyond the Rio Grande, and late information through Senr Cassiana & others, worthy of credit, is
positive in the fact that 16 hundred or two thousand troops
with good officers, well armed, and a plenty of provisions,
were on the point of marching (the provisions being cooked
&c) A detachment of active young men from volunteers under
my command have been sent out to the Rio Frio; they returned yesterday without information and we remain yet in
doubt whether they entend an attack on this place or go to
reinforce Matamoras. It does however seem certain that an attack is shortly to be made on this place & I think & it is the
general opinion that the enemy will come by land. The Citizens of Bejar have behaved well. Col. Neill & Myself have
come to the solemn resolution that we will rather die in these
ditches than give it up to the enemy. These citizens deserve
our protection and the public safety demands our lives rather
than to evacuate this post to the enemy — again we call aloud
for relief; the weakness of our post will at any rate bring the
enemy on, some volunteers are expected: Capt Patton with 5

147

or 6 has come in. But a large reinforcement with provisions is what we need.

"I have information just now from a friend whom I believe that the force at Rio Grande (Presidia) is two thousand complete; he states further that five thousand more is a little back and marching on, perhaps the 2 thousand will wait for a junction with the 5 thousand. This information is corroberated with all that we have heard. The informant says that they intend to make a descent on this place in particular, and there is no doubt of it.

"Our force is very small, the returns this day to the Comdt. is only one hundred and twenty officers and men. It would be a waste of men to put our brave little band against thousands.

"We have no interesting news to communicate. The army have elected two gentlemen to represent the Army & trust they will be received."

JAMES BOWIE
San Antonio de Bexar, Texas
2/2/1836[25]

"I have been in the field in actual duty for more than four Months and have not lost one hour from duty on account of sickness nor pleasure. But have served my country in every capacity I possibly could. when I left home it was with a determination to see Texas free & Independent sink or swim die or perish. And I have sanguine hopes of seeing my determination consumated. There is still a powerful force at Rio Grande say 2000 certain the last accounts we have is that they were preparing Ferry Boats to cross the River to march against us we know not when they may come. We are badly prepared to meet them. Though we will do the best we can.

"A great number of the volunteers here will leave tomorrow as the end of their second month is up and no pay no clothes nor no provisions — poor encouragement for patriotic men who have stood by their Country in the hour of trial. $7 each for 4 months We are now one hundred and fifty strong Col Crockett & Col Travis both here & Col Bowie in command of the volunteer forces. Col Neill left to day for home on account of an express from his family informing him of their ill health.[26]

"There was great regret at his departure by all of the men though he promised to be with us in 20 days at furtherest. We have nominated two delegates from the Army to represent us in the Convention which I hope will be received as we were not allowed the privilege of voting here they are both staunch Independence men & damn any other than such. I have some improved demonstrations to make & send you of our Fortress whereby fewer men & less Artillery will be required in case of a siege or an attack. Politics are all strait here and every man in the Army your friend. I have named to Genl Houston through col Neill & others that I would like a permanent appointment in the Engineer corps. And Know that my country will reward me as I may merit."

GREEN B. JAMESON
San Antonio de Bexar
2/11/1836[27]

"You have no doubt already received information, by Express from La Bahia, that tremendous preparations are making on the Rio Grande & elsewhere in the Interior for the Invasion of Texas — Santa Ana by the last accounts was at Saltillio, with a force of 2500 Men & Guns. Sesma was at the Rio Grande with about 2000 — He has issued his Proclamation denouncing vengence against the people of Texas. — and threatens to exterminate every white man within its limits — This being the Frontier Post nearest the Rio Grande, will be the first to be attacked. — We are illy prepared for their reception, as we have not more than 150 men here and they in a very disorganized state — Yet we are determined to sustain it as long as there is a man left; because we consider death preferable to disgrace, which would be the result of giving up a Post which has been so dearly won, and thus opening up the door for the Invaders to enter the sacred Territory of the Colonies. — We hope our countrymen will open their eyes to the present danger, and wake up from their false security — I hope that all party dissentions will subside, that our fellow

149

Citizens will unite in the Common Cause and fly to the defense of the Frontier.—

"I fear that it is useless to waste arguments upon them — The Thunder of the Enemy's Cannon and the pollution of their wives and daughters — The cries of their Famished Children, and the smoke of their burning dwellings, will only arouse them, — I regret that the Govt. has so long neglected a draft of the Militia, which is the only measure that will ever again bring the Citizens of Texas to the Frontiers.—

"Money, Clothing and Provisions are greatly needed at this Post for the use of the Soldiers.

"I hope your Excelly. will send us a portion of the money which has been received from the U.S. as it cannot be better applied, indeed we cannot get along any longer without Money: and with it we can do every thing.—

"For Gods sake, and the sake of our country, send us reinforcements — I hope you will send to this Post at least two companies of Regular Troops . . .

"In consequence of the sickness of his family, Lt. Col. Neill has left this Post, to visit home for a short time, and has requested me to take the Command of the Post. — In consequence of which, I feel myself delicately and awkwardly situated — I therefore hope that your Excelly will give me some definite orders, and that immediately —

"The Troops here, to a man, recognise you as their legitimate Govr, and they expect your fatherly care & protection. —

"In conclusion let me assure your Excelly, that with 200 more men I believe this place can be maintained & I hope they will be sent us as soon as possible Yet should we receive no reinforcements, I am determined to defend it to the last, and should Bejar fall, your friend will be buried beneath its ruins."

WILLIAM B. TRAVIS
San Antonio de Bexar, Texas
2/12/1836[28]

"Lt. Col. J. C. Neill being suddenly called home, in consequence of the illness of some of his family, requested Col. Travis, as the Senior officer, to assume the command of the

Post during his absence, — Col. Travis informed the volunteers in the Garrison, that they could, if not satisfied with him as a commandant Pro Tem, elect one out of their own body — The volunteers being under a wrong impression, and ever ready to catch at any popular excitement, objected to Col Travis upon the grounds of his being a Regular Officer, and immediately named Col Bowie as their choice.

"An election was consequently ordered by Col. Travis and Bowie was elected. — without opposition none but the volunteers voted & in fact not all of them — The consequence was a split in the Garrison. Col Travis, as a matter of course, would not submit to the control of Bowie and he (Bowie) availing himself of his popularity among the volunteers seemed anxious to arrogate to himself the entire control. —

"Things passed on this way yestarday & to-day until at length they have become intolerable — Bowie as Commandant of the volunteers, has gone so far as to stop carts Laden with the Goods of private families removing into the Country. He has ordered the Prison door to be opened for the release of a Mexican convicted of Theft who had been tried by a Jury of 12 men, among which was Col. Travis and Col. Bowie himself—

"He has also ordered, and effected, the release of D. H. Barre a private in the Regular army attached to the Legion of Cavalry, who had been tried by a court martial and found Guilty of mutiny, and actually liberated him from Prison with a Corporal Guard with Loud Huzzas. —

"But the most extraordinary step of all, & that which sets aside all Law, civil & military, is that which follows —

'Commandancy of Bejar Feby 13th 1836
Capts of co'ys.

You are hereby required to release such Prisoners as may be under your direction, for labour, or otherwise —
James Bowie
Commandant of the volunteer forces of Bejar'

"Under this order, the Mexicans who had been convicted by the civil authorities, and the soldiers convicted by Court-martials, & some of whom had been placed in the Alamo, on the public works, were released —

"Antonio Fuentes who had been released as above presented himself to the Judge under the protection of Capt. Baker of Bowies volunteers & demanded his Clothes which were in the Calaboose, Stating that Col. Bowie had set him at Liberty, whereupon the Judge (Seguin) ordered him to be remanded to prison, which was accordingly done, — As soon as this fact was reported to Bowie, he went, in a furious manner, and demanded of the Judge, a release of the Prisoner, which the Judge refused, saying that 'he would give up his office & let the military appoint a Judge' — Bowie immediately sent to the Alamo for troops and they immediately paraded in the Square, under arms, in a tumultuously and disorderly manner, Bowie, himself, and many of his men, being drunk which has been the case ever since he has been in command —

"Col Travis protested against the proceedings to the Judge, and others, and as a friend to good order, and anxious to escape the stigma which must inevitably follow, has, as a last resort, drawn off his Troops to the Medina, where he believes he may be as useful as in the Garrison, at all events, save himself from implication in this disgraceful business —

"I have ventured to give you a hasty sketch of passing events in justice to myself and others who have had no hand in this transaction."

JOHN J. BAUGH
San Antonio de Bexar, Texas
2/13/1836[29]

"I wrote you an official letter last night as Comdt of this Post in the absence of Col Neill; & if you had taken the trouble to answer my letter from Burnam's I should not now have been under the necessity of troubling you — My situation is truely awkward & delicate — Col Neill left me in the command — but wishing to give satisfaction to the volunteers here & not wishing to assume any command over them I issued an order for the election of an officer to command them with the exception of one company of volunteers that had previously engaged to serve under me. Bowie was elected by two small companey's; & since his election he has been roaring drunk all the time; has assumed all command — & is proceeding in a most disorderly & irregular manner — interfering with private property, releasing prisoners sentenced by court martial & by

152

the civil court & turning every thing topsy turvey — If I did not feel my honor & that of my country compromitted I would leave here instantly for some other point with the troops under my immediate command — as I am unwilling to be responsible for the drunken irregularities of any man. I hope you will immediately order some regular troops to this place — as it is more important to occupy this Post than I imagined when I last saw you — It is the key of Texas from the Interior without a footing here the enemy can do nothing against us in the colonies now that our coast is being guarded by armed vessels — I do not solicit the command of this post but as Col Neill has applied to the Commander in Chief to be relieved is anxious for me to take the command, I will do it if it be your order for a time until an artillery officer can be sent here. The citizens here have every confidence in me, as they can communicate with me, & they have shown every disposition to aid me with all they have — we need money — can you not send us some? I read your letter to the troops & they received it with acclamation — our spies have just returned from the Rio Grande — the enemy is there one thousand strong & is making every preperation to invade us. By the 15th of march I think Texas will be invaded & every preparation should be made to receive them . . .

"In conclusion, allow me to beg that you will give me definite orders immediately."

WILLIAM B. TRAVIS
San Antonio de Bexar
2/13/1836[30]

"I am glad to learn that you are in good health and spirits. — Be assured Sir that the country will sustain you. — We are unanimous in your favor here and determined to have nothing to do with that corrupt council. — It is my duty to inform you that my department is nearly destitute of medicine and in the event of a siege I can be very little use to the sick under such circumstances — I have plenty of instruments with the exception of a trephining-case, some catheters and an injection syringe which would complete this station. — I write you this because I suppose the Surgeon general not to be in

153

the country and we are threatened by a large invading army. — Four Mexicans are to represent this Jurisdiction in the convention although we might with great ease have sent the same number of Americans, had it not have been that a few of our people through Mexican policy perfectly hoodwinked headquarters, making them believe that it was unjust to attempt to send any other than Mexicans, thereby, exerting all that influence to the same end. — Perhaps I have said enough. However, I intend that those representatives shall distinctly understand, previous to their leaving, that if they vote against independence, they will have to be very careful on returning here. I wish Gen. Houston was now on the frontier to help us crush at once both our external and internal enemies. — Let us show them how republicans can and will fight.

P.S. Some method should be devised to neutralize Fannin's influence."

AMOS POLLARD
San Antonio de Bexar, Texas
2/13/1836[31]

"I wrote you from Gonzales and soon after left there for this place, yet under different views from what I stated in as a sudden attack was expected on our garrison here and were called on for assistance. It is however fully ascertained that we have nothing of the kind to apprehend before a month or six weeks as the Enemy have not yet crossed the Rio Grande 180 mi. distant from this place nor are they expected to make any movement this way until the weather becomes warm or until the grass is sufficiently up to support their horses we conceive it however important to be prepared as a heavy attack is expected from Santa Ana himself in the Spring as no doubt the despot will use every possible means and strain every nerve to conquer and exterminate us from the land — in this we have no fear and are confident that Texas cannot only sustain what she now holds but take Mexico itself did she think on conquest . . .

"We want men who can undergo hardships and deprivation. Otherwise they are only a pest and expense to their fellow Soldiers . . .

"I say come on, there is a fine field open to you all no

matter how you are situated or what may be your circumstances. At least come and see the country, as a farmer, mechanic or a Soldier you will do well — I believe no country offers such strong inducements to Emmigration . . . I am to leave this to return to the Cibilo Creek in company with 10 others to take up, our lands we get as citizens which in more than 1100 acres for single men, men of family 4428 acres our volunteer pay is 20$ per month & 640 acres at close of war . . .

"It might be that I might be of some benefit to you here provided any of you could have a mind to come out and indeed to speak sincearly this would be the Country for us all, nothing could induce me from my determination of settling here, . . .

"As I will most likely be engaged in surveying of public lands I might be of service to some of our friends in procurring disirable or choice locations."

DAVID P. CUMMINGS
San Antonio de Bexar, Texas
2/14/1836[32]

"We had detained Mr. Williams for the purpose of saying that the Garrison is in a very destitute situation we have but a small supply of provisions and we are without a dollar. We therefore beg leave to call the attention of your Excellency to the wants of this post, as we learn that 20,000 dollars have been sent to Copeno for the use of the Troops there. We think it but just that you should send us at least 5000 dollars which we understand you have at your command.

"We have borrowed 500 dollars here, which has long since been Expended, and besides which we are greatly in debt and our credit is growing worse daily. It is useless to talk of keeping up the garrison any longer without money as we believe that unless we receive some shortly the men will all leave.

"From all the information we have received there is no doubt but that the enemy will shortly advance upon this place, and that this will be the first point of attack we must therefore urge the necessity of sending reinforcements, as speedily as possible to our aid.

"By an understanding of to day Col. J. Bowie has the

command of the volunteers of the garrison, and Col. W. B. Travis of the regulars and volunteer cavalry.

"All general orders and corrispondence will henceforth be signed both until Col. Neills return."

WILLIAM B. TRAVIS
JAMES BOWIE
San Antonio de Bexar, Texas
2/14/1836[33]

"I have been dilatory in communicating to you the situation as well as the plan of the Fortress . . . But will now send you a complete plan of the same showing its situation at the time it was surrendered to us. Also such improvements as we have made . . . erecting redoubts digging wells & mounting cannon . . . But after seeing the improbability & perhaps the impractibility and impolicy of keeping up a strong Garrison here, I now submit a further suggestion . . . The suggestion is, to square the Alamo and erect a large redoubt at each corner supported by Bastions & leave a ditch all around full of water. when squared in that way four cannon & fewer men would do more effective service than twenty pieces of artillery does or can do in the way they are now mounted. The mexicans have shown imbecility and want of skill in this Fortress as they have done in all things else — I have seen many fortifications in the U.S. and find that all of the Interior ones are square and those of the Forts are generally circular —

"Taking into consideration the scarsity of Tools we have done well in mounting & remounting Guns and other necessary work — If I were ordered to construct a new & effective Fortress on an economical plan I would suggest a diamond with two acute & two obtuse angles — with few men & Guns with a sufficient entrenchment all around such a Fortress with projecting redoubts & Bastions would command all points . . . I beg leave to tender to you my high esteem for your firm & unshaken course pursued since you have had the honor to preside over this state . . . and also that of the Garrison."

GREEN B. JAMESON
San Antonio de Bexar, Texas
2/16/1836[34]

"The enemy in large force is in sight. We want men and provisions. Send them to us. We have 150 men and are determined to defend the Alamo to the last. Give us assistance.

"P.S. Send an express to San Felipe with news night and day."

WILLIAM B. TRAVIS
The Alamo
2/23/1836[35]

"To the People of Texas & all Americans in the world — Fellow citizens and Compatriots — I am besieged by a thousand or more of the Mexicans under Santa Anna. I have sustained a continual Bombardment & cannonade for 24 hours & have not lost a man. The enemy has demanded a surrender at discretion, otherwise, the garrison are to be put to the sword, if the fort is taken. I have answered the demand with a cannon shot, & our flag still waves proudly from the walls. I shall never surrender or retreat. Then, I call on you in the name of Liberty, of patriotism & everything dear to the American character to come to our aid with all dispatch. The enemy is receiving reinforcements daily & will no doubt increase to three or four thousand in four or five days. If this call is neglected, I am determined to sustain myself as long as possible & die like a soldier who never forgets what is due his own honor & that of his country. VICTORY or DEATH.
P.S. The Lord is on our side. When the enemy appeared in sight we had not three bushels of corn. We have since found in deserted houses 80 to 90 bushels and got into the walls 20 or 30 head of Beeves."

WILLIAM B. TRAVIS
The Alamo
2/24/1836[36]

"In a few words there is 2000 Mexican soldiers in Bexar, and 150 Americans in the Alamo. Sesma is at the head of them, and from the best accounts that can be obtained, they intend to show no quarter. If every man cannot turn out to a man every man in the Alamo will be murdered.

"They have not more than 8 or 10 days provision. They

say they will defend it or die on the ground. Provisions, ammunition and Men, or you suffer your men to be murdered in the Fort. If you do not turn out Texas is gone. I left Bexar on the 23rd. at 4 P.M."

LAUNCELOT SMITHER
Gonzales, Texas
2/24/1836[37]

"Since the above was writen I heard a very heavy Canonade during the whole day think there must have been an attack made upon the Alamo We were short of Ammunition when I left. Hurry on all the men you can in haste.

"When I left there was but 150 determined to do or die tomorrow I leave for Bejar with what men I can raise."

ALBERT MARTIN
Gonzales, Texas
2/25/1836[38]

"I hope Every one will Randeves at gonzales as soon as poseble as the Brave Soldiers are suffering do not neglect powder is very scarce and should not be delad one moment."

LAUNCELOT SMITHER
Gonzales, Texas
2/25/1836[39]

"On the 23rd of Feb. the enemy in large force entered the city of Bexar, which could not be prevented, as I had not sufficient forces to occupy both positions. Col. Batres, the Adjutant-Major of the President-General Santa Anna, demanded a surrender at discretion, calling us foreign rebels. I answered them with a cannon shot, upon which the enemy commenced a bombardment with a five-inch howitzer, which together with a heavy cannonade, has been kept up incessantly ever since. I instantly sent express to Col. Fannin, at Goliad, and to the people of Gonzales and San Felipe. Today at 10 o'clock A.M. some two or three hundred Mexicans crossed the river below and came up under cover of the houses until they arrived within point blank shot, when we opened a heavy discharge of grape and cannister on them, together with a well directed fire from small arms which forced them to halt and take shelter in the houses 90 or 100 yards from our batteries. The action continued to rage about two hours, when the enemy retreated in confusion, dragging off many of their dead and wounded.

"During the action the enemy kept up a constant bombardment and discharge of balls, grape and canister. We knew from actual observation that many of the enemy were wounded — while we, on our part, have not lost a man. Two or three of our men have been slightly scratched by pieces of rock, but have not been disabled. I take great pleasure in stating that both officers and men conducted themselves with firmness and bravery. Lieutenant Simmons of cavalry acting as infantry, and Captains Carey, Dickinson and Blair of the artillery, rendered essential service, and Charles Despallier and Robert Brown gallantly sallied out and set fire to houses which afforded the enemy shelter, in the face of enemy fire. Indeed, the whole of the men who were brought into action, conducted themselves with such undaunted heroism that it would be injustice to discriminate. The Hon. David Crockett was seen at all points animating the men to do their duty. Our numbers are few and the enemy still continues to approximate his works to ours. I have every reason to apprehend an attack from his whole force very soon; but I shall hold out to the last extremity, hoping to secure reinforcements in a day or two. Do hasten on aid to me as rapidly as possible, as from the superior number of the enemy, it will be impossible for us to keep them out much longer. If they overpower us, we fall a sacrifice at the shrine of our country, and we hope posterity and our country will do our memory justice. Give me help, oh my Country! Victory or Death!"

WILLIAM B. TRAVIS
The Alamo
2/25/1836[40]

"I have this moment, 8 p.m., arrived from Bexar. On the 23d, I was requested by Colonel Travis to take Lieutenant Nobles and reconnoitre the enemy. Some distance out I met a

Mexican who informed me that the town had been invested. After a short time a messenger overtook me, saying he had been sent by a friend of my wife to let me know that it would be impossible for me to return, as two large bodies of Mexican troops were already around the town. I then proceeded to the Rovia and remained till 10 p.m., on the 25th. On the 24th there was heavy cannonading, particularly at the close of the evening. I left the Rovia at 10 p.m., on the 25th, and heard no more firing, from which I conclude the Alamo had been taken by storm. On the night of the 24th, I was informed that there were from four to six thousand Mexicans in and around Bexar."

PHILIP DIMITT
Dimitt's Point, Texas
2/28/1836[41]

"Do me the favor to send the enclosed to its proper destination instantly. I am still here, in fine spirits and well to do. With 140 men, I have held this place 10 days against a force variously estimated from 1,500 to 6,000, and I shall continue to hold it till I get relief from my countrymen, or I will perish in its defense. We have had a shower of bombs and cannon balls continually falling among us the whole time, yet none of us have fallen. We have been miraculously preserved. You have no doubt seen my official report of the action of the 25th ult. in which we repulsed the enemy with considerable loss; on the night of the 25th they made another attempt to charge us in the rear of the fort; but we received them gallantly by a discharge of grape shot and musquetry, and they took to their scrapers immediately. They are now encamped under entrenchments, on all sides of us.

"All our couriers have gotten out without being caught, and a company of 32 men from Gonzales got in two nights ago, and Col. Bonham got in to-day by coming between the powder house and the enemy's upper encampment. Let the Convention go on and make a declaration of independence; and we will then understand, and the world will understand what we are fighting for. If independece is not declared, I shall lay down my arms, and so will the men under my com-

160

mand. But under the flag of independence, we are ready to peril our lives a hundred times a day, and dare the monster who is fighting us under a blood red flag. Threatening to murder all prisoners and make Texas a waste desert. I shall have to fight the enemy on his own terms; yet I am ready to do it, and if my countrymen do not rally to my relief, I am determined to perish in the defense of this place, and my bones shall reproach my country for her neglect. With 500 men more, I will drive Sesma beyond the Rio Grande, and I will visit my vengence on the enemy of Texas whether invaders or resident Mexican enemies. All the citizens of this place that have not joined us are with the enemy fighting against us. Let the government declare them public enemies, otherwise she is acting a suicidal part. I shall treat them as such, unless I have superior orders to the contrary. My respects to all friends, confusion to all enemies. God bless you."

WILLIAM B. TRAVIS
The Alamo
3/3/1836[42]

"In the present confusion of the political authorities of the country, and in absence of the commander-in-chief, I beg leave to communicate to you the situation of this garrison . . .

"From the twenty-fifth to the present date the enemy have kept up a bombardment from two howitzers, one a five and a half inch, and the other an eight inch, — and a heavy cannonade from two long nine-pounders, mounted on a battery on the opposite side of the river, at a distance of four hundred yards from our wall. During this period the enemy have been busily employed in encircling us in with entrenched encampments on all sides, at the following distances, to wit: In Bexar, four hundred yards west; in Lavillita, three hundred yards south; at the powder-house, one thousand yards east of south; on the ditch, eight hundred yards northeast, and at the old mill, eight hundred yards north. Notwithstanding all this, a company of thirty-two men from Gonzales, made their way in to us on the morning of the first inst. at three o'clock, and Colonel J. B. Bonham (a courier from Gonzales) got in this morning at eleven o'clock without molestation. I have fortified this place, so that the walls are generally proof against cannon balls; I shall continue to entrench on the inside, and strengthen the walls by throwing up dirt. At least two hundred shells have fallen inside of our works without having injured a single man; indeed we have been so fortunate as not to lose a man from any cause, and we have killed many of the enemy. The spirits of my men are still high although they have had much to depress them. We have contended for ten days against an enemy whose numbers are variously estimated from fifteen hundred to six thousand men, with General Ramirez-Sesma and Colonel Batres, the aid-de-camp of Santa Anna, at their head. A report was circulated that Santa Anna himself was with the enemy, but I think it was false. A reinforcement of about one thousand men is now entering Bexar from the west and I think it more probable that Santa Anna is now in town, from the rejoicing we hear.

"Col. Fannin is said to be on the march to this place with reinforcements but I fear it is not true, as I have repeatedly sent to him for aid without receiving any. Colonel Bonham, my special messenger, arrived at La Bahia fourteen days ago, with a request for aid, and on the arrival of the enemy in Bexar, ten days ago, I sent an express to Colonel F., which arrived at Goliad on the next day, urging him to send us reinforcements; none have yet arrived. I look to the colonies alone for aid; unless it arrives soon, I shall have to fight the enemy on his own terms. I will, however, do the best I can under the circumstances; and I feel confident that the determined valor and desperate courage, heretofore exhibited by my men, will not fail them in the last struggle; and although they may be sacrificed to the vengence of a Gothic enemy, the victory will cost the enemy so dear, that it will be worse for him than defeat. I hope your honorable body will hasten on reinforcements, ammunitions and provisions to our aid so soon as possible. We have provisions for twenty days for the men we have. Our supply of ammunition is limited. At least five hundred pounds of cannon powder, and two hundred rounds of six, nine, twelve and eighteen pound balls, ten kegs of rifle powder and a supply of lead should be sent to this place without delay, under a sufficient guard.

"If these things are promptly sent and large reinforcements are hastened to this frontier, this neighborhood will be the great and decisive ground. The power of Santa Anna is to be met here or in the colonies; we had better meet them here than to suffer a war of devastation to rage in our settlements. A blood red banner waves from the church of Bejar, and in the camp above us, in token that the war is one of vengence against rebels; they have declared us as such; demanded that we should surrender at discretion, or that this garrison should be put to the sword. Their threats have no influence on me or my men, but to make all fight with desperation and that high-souled courage that characterizes the patriot who is willing to die in defence of his country's liberty and his own honor.

"The citizens of this municipality are all our enemies, except those who have joined us heretofore. We have three Mexicans now in the fort; those who have not joined us in this extremity, should be declared public enemies, and their property should aid in paying the expenses of the war.

"The bearer of this will give your honorable body a statement more in detail, should he escape through the enemy's lines.

"God and Texas — Victory or Death."

WILLIAM B. TRAVIS
The Alamo
3/3/1836[43]

"Take care of my little boy. If the country should be saved, I may make him a splendid fortune; but if the country should be lost and I should perish, he will have nothing but the proud recollection that he is the son of a man who died for his country."

WILLIAM B. TRAVIS
The Alamo
3/3/1836[44]

"These remains, which we have had the honor to carry on our shoulders, are the remains of those valient heroes who died at the Alamo. Yes, my friends, they preferred to die a thousand times than to live under the yoke of a tyrannt.

163

"What a brillant example! One worthy of inclusion in the pages of history. From her throne above, the spirit of liberty appears to look upon us, and with tearful countenance points, saying 'Behold your brothers, Travis, Bowie, Crockett as well as all the others. Their valour has earned them a place with all my heros.'

"Yes, fellow soldiers and fellow citizens, we are witness to the meritorious acts of those who, when faced with a reversal in fortune, during the late contest, chose to offer their lives to the ferocity of the enemy. A barbarous enemy who on foot herded them like animals to this spot, and then proceeded to reduce them to ashes.

"I invite all of you to join me in holding the venerable remains of our worthy companions before the eyes of the entire world to show it that Texas shall be free, and independent. Or, to a man, we will die gloriously in combat."

JUAN N. SEGUIN
San Antonio de Bexar, Texas
2/25/1837[45]

"You ask me if I remember it. I tell you yes. It is burned into my brain and indelibly seared there. Neither age nor infirmity could make me forget."

ENRIQUE ESPARZA
San Antonio, Texas
1907[46]

164

Notes

Preface

1. Quote by Mardell Plainfeather. Robert P. Jordan, "Ghosts on the Little Bighorn," *National Geographic Magazine* 170, no. 6 (December 1986):813.

2. Walter Lord, *A Time to Stand* (New York: Harper & Row, 1961), 200.

3. Amelia M. Williams, "A Critical Study of the Siege of the Alamo and the Personnel of Its Defenders," *Southwestern Historical Quarterly* 37, no. 4 (April 1934):286–303.

4. William F. Gray compiled a list of Alamo casualties in his diary, dated 3/20/1836, two weeks after the Alamo battle took place. Another list, with some variations, appeared in the *Telegraph and Texas Register* four days later. William F. Gray, *From Virginia to Texas* (Houston: Gray, Dillaye & Co., 1909; reprint, Houston: Fletcher Young Publishing Co., 1965), 138 (page references are to reprint edition); and *San Felipe (Texas) Telegraph and Texas Register*, 3/24/1836, 143.

5. Walter Lord explains the death of Sherod Dover, thought to be an Alamo defender, in *A Time to Stand*, 213.

6. Information on previously unknown Alamo defender Damacio Ximenes is only now coming to light. Karen Malkowski, "New Hero of the Alamo Discovered," *San Antonio Express News*, 9/13/1986, 1C, p. 1.

Part I

1. From a poem by Grantland Rice, in *New York Tribune*, 1916, reprinted in Adina de Zavala, *The Alamo: Where the Last Man Died* (San Antonio, Naylor Co., 1956), 55.

2. The siege and battle of Bexar was the campaign in which Texan forces defeated Mexican General Martín Perfecto de Cos in San Antonio de Bexar and at the Alamo in November and December of 1835, temporarily driving the Mexican army from Texas and setting the stage for the siege and battle of the Alamo.

The town of San Antonio de Bexar, now the present-day city of San Antonio, Texas, was commonly known as Bexar, and will be referred to as such in this work.

3. Rueben Marmaduke Potter (1802–1890) did the first in-depth study of the Alamo battle in 1860 and revised it in 1876. See Williams, "A Critical Study," 243; and Rueben M. Potter, "The Fall of the Alamo," *Magazine of American History,* January 1878; reprint, Rueben M. Potter, *The Fall of the Alamo* (Hillsdale, NJ: Otterden Press, 1977).

4. Erastus Smith (1787–1837), better known as "Deaf" Smith, was a famed Texan scout and highly regarded soldier of the Texas Revolution.

5. The battle of San Jacinto (4/21/1836) was the decisive battle of the Texas Revolution. Gen. Sam Houston defeated Mexican General Santa Anna, taking him prisoner and ensuring Texan independence from Mexico.

6. Generalissimo Antonio López de Santa Anna (1794–1876) was the ruler of Mexico, commander of the Mexican forces in Texas in 1836, and conqueror of the Alamo.

7. Comptroller Military Service Record, no. 74. See Williams, "A Critical Study," 243.

8. Frank Templeton, *Margaret Ballentine or the Fall of the Alamo* (Houston: State Printing Co., 1907), noted in Williams, "A Critical Study," 244.

9. John S. Ford, *Origin and Fall of the Alamo* (San Antonio: Johnson Bros. Printing, 1900; reprint, Austin: Shelby Publishers, 1980), 26 (page references are to reprint edition); and José M. Rodriguez, *Memoirs of Early Texas* (San Antonio: Standard Printing, 1961).

10. James C. Neill (1790–1845) was a lieutenant colonel of artillery in the Texan army and commander of the post at Bexar after the Texan forces drove the Mexican army out, in December 1835. Neill turned over command of the post to Lt. Col. William B. Travis in early February 1836, while he attempted to obtain much needed money and supplies for the garrison. He was unable to return to the Alamo before its fall, and was later wounded in the battle of San Jacinto.

11. The Volunteer Auxiliary Corps of Texas was made up of recent arrivals in Texas, mostly from the United States. They enlisted for a period of at least three months, received less land bounty than those enlisted in the Permanent Volunteers, for the duration of the war, and they were able to elect their own company officers. See Eugene C. Barker, "The Texan Revolutionary Army," *Quarterly of the Texas State Historical Association* 9, no. 4 (April 1906):233–34.

12. NCO refers to noncommisioned officer.

13. VAC refers to Volunteer Auxiliary Corps.

14. Daniel W. Cloud to J. B. Cloud, 12/26/1835, *San Antonio Express*, 11/24/1901; typescript in Daniel W. Cloud file, DRT Library at the Alamo, San Antonio.

15. The Gonzales Ranging Company of Mounted Volunteers were citizens of the town of Gonzales who were mustered into service by Byrd Lockhart on 2/23/1836. They comprised the nucleus of the relief force which rode from Gonzales to reinforce the Alamo. For the purposes of this book, the Gonzales Ranging Company, as it will be called, will refer to this original group, plus others who joined them just before they left for the Alamo. See Daughters of the Republic of Texas, *Muster Rolls of the Texas Revolution* (Austin, 1986), 25.

16. Williams, "A Critical Study," 246.

17. Henry Smith (1788–1851) was appointed the political chief of the Brazos Department in 1834 by the Mexican governor of Coahuila and Texas. He became one of the leaders of the Texas independence movement and was named governor of Texas by the provisional government at the outset of the Revolution. He served as the chief executive of Texas for the duration of the Revolution.

18. John J. Baugh to Henry Smith, 2/13/1836, John H. Jenkins. ed., *Papers of the Texas Revolution 1835–1836* (Austin, Presidial Press, 1973), 4:320–21.

19. Stephen F. Austin (1793–1836) was the foremost leader and colonizer of Anglo-American Texas. During the early stages of the Texas Revolution, he was elected to command the volunteer troops against the Mexican forces at Bexar.

20. The battle of Concepcion took place about one mile from the mission Nuestra Señora de la Purisima Concepcion, just south of Bexar. A ninety-man detachment under James Bowie and James W. Fannin stood off an attack of about 400 Mexican cavalrymen from a defensive position along the San Antonio River.

21. James W. Fannin, Jr. (1804–1836) was the Texan commander of the garrison at Goliad, about ninety miles southeast of Bexar.

22. William H. Patton (1808–1842) was captain of a group of ten volunteers who arrived at Bexar on 1/18/1836. He left Bexar upon the arrival of the Mexican army, but later took part in the battle of San Jacinto.

23. Proceedings of the Nacogdoches Board of Land Commissioners, Claim #254, by the heirs of John Blair, noted in R. B. Blake, "A Vindication of Rose and His Story," in *In the Shadow of History*, ed. J. Frank Dobie, Mody C. Boatright, and Harry H. Ran-

som, Texas Folklore Society Publications, no. 15 (Austin: Texas Folklore Society, 1939; reprint, Detroit: Folklore Associates, 1971), 32 (page references are to reprint edition).

24. Sam Houston of Tennessee was the commander of the Texan forces during the Texas Revolution.

25. James B. Bonham to Sam Houston, 12/1/1835, Jenkins, *Papers*, 3:61.

26. *El Nacional* (Mexico City), Suplemento al Numero 79, 1836. Copy in the Barker Texas History Center, University of Texas, Austin.

27. Election returns, 11/24/1835. Jenkins, *Papers*, 2:496.

28. The Matamoros Expedition was a plan by the Consultation of Texas to invade the Mexican town of Matamoros, occupy it, and use it as a base of operations against the Mexican army in Mexico. See Sam Houston's orders to James Bowie, 12/7/1835, Jenkins, *Papers*, 3:222.

29. Sam Houston to Henry Smith, 1/17/1836, Jenkins, *Papers*, 4:46.

30. James Bowie to Henry Smith, 2/2/1835 [1836], Jenkins, *Papers*, 4:236.

31. Baugh to Smith, Jenkins, *Papers*, 4:320–21; and William B. Travis to Henry Smith, 2/13/1836, Jenkins, *Papers*, 327–28.

32. Despite popular legend which portrays him as a hard and abusive drinker, contemporary accounts state that Bowie was unusually temperate for his times. Even though he would have a drink occasionally, he would rarely be seen drunk. See Williams, "A Critical Study," 103.

33. The exact nature of Bowie's debilitating illness is uncertain. It is usually described as "typhoid-pneumonia." See Williams, "A Critical Study," 102.

34. *Ibid.*

35. La Villita was a section of small huts and houses across the San Antonio River from Bexar proper, and just south of the Alamo.

36. Williams, "A Critical Study," 250–52; and Sherman to Harrison, 4/24/1836, Jenkins, *Papers*, 6:51.

37. The fight for the Gonzales cannon (10/2/1835) has been called the "Lexington of Texas," since it was the opening battle of the Texas Revolution. A small Mexican force under Lieutenant Castañeda was sent from Bexar to Gonzales to retrieve a small cannon, given to the town four years before, for protection against Indians. When the Mexican troops demanded the cannon, the Texan settlers resisted and unfurled a flag with the legend, "Come and Take It." After the ensuing fight, the Mexican troops were driven back to Bexar without the cannon.

38. Ralph W. Steen, "Letter from San Antonio de Bexar in 1836," *Southwestern Historical Quarterly* 62:513–18; and William R. Carey to brothers and sister, 1/12/1836, Jenkins, *Papers,* 3:494.

39. Claim by Moses Carey for pay due William R. Carey, 6/25/1839, Archives Division, Texas State Library, Austin.

40. Blake, "Vindication of Rose," 34.

41. Two weeks after the Alamo battle, the Goliad garrison under Fannin was caught in the open by a Mexican force under General Urrea and forced to surrender on 3/20/1836. One week later, approximately 400 of these prisoners were executed following Santa Anna's policy of "no quarter."

42. John Sutherland, "The Fall of the Alamo," in James T. DeShields. *Tall Men with Long Rifles* (San Antonio, Naylor, 1935; reprint 1971), 160–61 (page references are to reprint edition).

43. *Ibid.*

44. Wlliam B. Travis to Sam Houston, 2/25/1836, printed in Jenkins, *Papers,* 4:433.

45. A controversy continues to rage over Crockett's death. Although current popular opinion favors the theory that Crockett was one of five to seven prisoners taken during the battle and then executed on the orders of Santa Anna, there is at least as much, if not more, evidence to support his dying in combat, as opposed to his being executed.

However, a national hero failing to live up to his legendary status is fertile ground, commercially, so only one side of the story has received much press. A realistic evaluation of various accounts supports Crockett's death in combat. At the very least there is enough evidence to leave the question open. The accounts which support the capture and execution are at best circumstantial and in no way constitute proof beyond a reasonable doubt. Unfortunately, these theories have more financial than historical value, so until both sides of the story receive equal attention, the stories of Crockett's execution will be with us for quite a while. See Bill Groneman, "The Death of Davy Crockett," in *Roll Call at the Alamo,* by Phil Rosenthal and Bill Groneman (Fort Collins, CO: Old Army Press, 1985), 29.

46. John Gadsby Chapman quoted in Curtis C. Davis, "A Legend at Full Length — Mr. Chapman Paints Colonel Crockett — and Tells About It," *American Antiquarian Society Proceedings* 69, part 2 (October 1959): 155–74; and Richard Boyd Hauck, *Crockett: A Bio-Bibliography* (Westport, CT: Greenwood Press, 1982), 63.

47. For more detailed descriptions of Crockett see James A. Shackford, *David Crockett: The Man and the Legend* (Chapel Hill, NC: University of North Carolina Press, 1956; reprint, Westport, CT:

Greenwood Press, 1981), 282–83 (page references are to reprint edition); Hauck, *Crockett: A Bio-Bibliography*, 50–54, 60–67, 90–91, 107–113; and Frederick S. Voss, "Portraying an American Original: The Likenesses of Davy Crockett," *Southwestern Historical Quarterly* 91, no. 4 (April 1988): 457–482.

48. John Gadsby Chapman, *David Crockett*, oil on canvas, n.d., Iconography Collection, Harry Ransom Humanities Research Center, University of Texas, Austin.

49. James W. Fannin to Francis DeSauque and John Chenworth, 3/1/1836, Army Papers, Archives Division, Texas State Library, Austin, printed in Jenkins, *Papers*, 4:477–78.

50. William B. Travis to Sam Houston, 2/25/1836, *Little Rock Arkansas Gazette*, 4/12/1836, printed in Jenkins, *Papers*, 4:433–34.

51. Richard C. King, *Susanna Dickinson — Messenger of the Alamo* (Austin: Shoal Creek, 1976), 2.

52. DeShields, *Tall Men with Long Rifles*, 190.

53. Susannah [Dickerson] Hannig, in J. M. Morphis, *History of Texas* (New York: United States Publishing Co., 1875), 176.

54. *Bellows v. Bellows*, H. 479 (11th Judicial Court of Harris County, 1857) cited in King, *Susanna Dickinson*, 70.

55. "The Survivor of the Alamo," *San Antonio Daily Express*, 4/28/1881.

56. Stephen F. Austin to Philip Dimitt, 11/18/1835, *Quarterly of the Texas State Historical Association* 11:47–48, printed in Jenkins, *Papers*, 2:448.

57. The Goliad Declaration, *Brazoria Texas Republican*, 1/13/1836, printed in Jenkins, *Papers*, 3:265–70.

58. Houston to Smith, 1/17/1836.

59. DeShields, *Tall Men with Long Rifles*, 160.

60. Sam Houston to Philip Dimitt, 3/12/1836, A. J. Houston Papers, Archives Division, Texas State Library, Austin, printed in Jenkins, *Papers*, 5:57–58.

61. Enrique Esparza, "Story of the Massacre of Heroes of the Alamo," *San Antonio Express*, 3/7/1905; and "Alamo's Only Survivor," *San Antonio Express*, 5/12 and 5/19/1907.

62. *Ibid.*

63. *Ibid.*

64. Although there is no documented proof, evidence indicates that defenders with families present in the Alamo were assigned battle positions in close proximity to their families. This seems to have been the case with Esparza, Dickerson, and Anthony Wolf.

65. Clifford White, *1830 Citizens of Texas* (Austin: Eakin Publications, 1983), 103.

66. Williams, "Critical Study," 258.

67. The Texan army of 1835 and 1836 was made up of a regular army, consisting of regular troops enlisted for two years and permanent volunteers enlisted for the duration of the war; a militia, with companies organized within each municipality; and a Volunteer Auxiliary Corps of recent arrivals in Texas. See Walter Prescott Webb, ed., *The Handbook of Texas* (Austin: Texas State Historical Association, 1952), 1:69–70; and Barker, "Texan Revolutionary Army," 227–61.

68. Don L. Fuqua, Iowa to Lois Lentz, Texas, October 29, December 3, and December 30, 1975, Fuqua file, DRT Library at the Alamo.

69. Albert Curtis, *Remember the Alamo Heroes* (San Antonio: Clegg Co., 1961), 9.

70. Court of Claims voucher #1824, file (E-G), Texas General Land Office; noted in Williams, "A Critical Study," 260–61.

71. Ana Salazar Esparza may have been born Maria Josefa Ana Estacia Salazar on 1/23/1813, in Bexar. The maiden name of this child's mother was Gonzales. Her paternal grandmother was also named Gonzales. Her godmother's name was Maria Petra Sais, possibly "Doña Petra," to a small child. Baptismal Record of the San Fernando Church, 1/23/1813, San Antonio.

72. Cornett was an officer rank below that of lieutenant. This rank of the British army was apparently adopted by the newly formed Texan army. A cornett was the guidon bearer of his unit.

73. John C. Goodrich to Sam Houston, 11/28/1835, A. J. Houston Papers, Archives Division, Texas State Library, printed in Jenkins, *Papers,* 3:15.

74. DRT, *Muster Rolls,* 42.

75. The Alamo *acequia* was an irrigation ditch which supplied water to the Alamo.

76. Pension Claims, P.C. no 996, 11/2/1874, Archives Division, Texas State Library, Austin.

77. File Milam, Donation no. 1109, Texas General Land Office, quoted in Thomas L. Miller, "Mexican-Texans at the Alamo," *Journal of Mexican-American History* 2, no. 1 (Fall 1971):35.

78. File Robertson Bounty no. 1064, quoted in Miller, "Mexican-Texans."

79. Miller, "Mexican-Texans," 35.

80. The Grass Fight took place on 11/26/1835 as part of the siege of Bexar, when a Texan force under James Bowie intercepted a Mexican pack train thought to be carrying pay and reinforcements for the Mexican troops in Bexar. After a short battle, the Texans dis-

covered the pack train to have been carrying grass for the horses of the Mexican garrison.

81. Green Jameson to Sam Houston, 1/18/1836, Jenkins, *Papers,* 4:58–61.

82. Robert E. Davis. ed., *Diary of William Barret Travis* (Waco: Texian Press, 1966), 127.

83. Gray, *From Virginia to Texas,* 136–38.

84. *Houston Telegraph and Texas Register,* May 26 through August 1837; printed in David Drake, " 'Joe' Alamo Hero," *Negro History Bulletin* (April–May–June 1981).

85. Williams, "A Critical Study," 285–86.

86. See *San Felipe (Texas) Telegraph and Texas Register,* 3/24/1836; Gray, *From Virginia to Texas,* 138–42; Chester Newell, *History of the Revolution in Texas* (New York: Wiley & Putnam, 1838; reprint, New York: Arno Press, 1973), 211–12 (page references are to reprint edition); and DRT, *Muster Rolls,* 25–27.

87. There were other slaveholders among the Alamo garrison, such as Micajah Autry, Mial Scurlock, and possibly William R. Carey. Any one of them, plus any of the other defenders, may have had a slave at the Alamo. See Gray, *From Virginia to Texas,* 137.

88. Curtis, *Remember the Alamo Heroes,* 33.

89. The Fredonian Movement was a wild scheme by a small group of men to form an alliance with Texas Indian tribes, overthrow Mexican rule, and divide Texas between the tribes and the independent republic of "Fredonia." It began in mid-December of 1826 and ended in late January of 1827, when Texan militia led by Mexican officers drove the revolutionaries from Texas.

90. G. A. McCall, "William T. Malone," *Quarterly of the Texas State Historical Association* 14, no. 4 (April 1911):325–26.

91. Michael R. Green, "To the People of Texas and All Americans in the World," *Southwestern Historical Quarterly* 91, no. 4 (April 1988):500.

92. "Testimony of Mrs. Hannig touching the Alamo Massacre, Sept. 23, 1876," Adjutant General's Letters Concerning the Alamo, Archives Division, Texas State Library, Austin.

93. Lord, *A Time to Stand,* 161.

94. The Texas Consultation was a meeting of Texan delegates, which convened from October to November of 1835, to decide on what course of action Texas should take in response to the dictatorship of Santa Anna. See Webb, ed., *Handbook of Texas,* 1:403.

95. Gregory Curtis, "Forgery Texas Style," *Texas Monthly* (March 1989):105.

96. Esparza, "Story of the Massacre," n.p.; Gray, *From Virginia*

to Texas, 137; and Jake Ivey, "The Losoyas and the Texas Revolution," *Alamo Lore and Myth Organization Newsletter* 4, no. 1 (March 1982):12.

97. Curtis, *Remember the Alamo Heroes,* 56.

98. The battle of Velasco took place on 6/26/1832 between Texan and Mexican forces, when the Texans sought to transport a cannon from Brazoria to use against the Mexican force at Anahuac. The confrontation occurred at Fort Velasco as the Mexican commander, Domingo de Ugartechea, tried to prevent the Texans from transporting the cannon down the Brazos River. In the ensuing battle, the Mexican troops ran out of ammunition and were forced to surrender.

99. Sam Houston to Henry Smith, 1/17/1836, Army Papers, Archives Division, Library of the University of Texas, Austin, printed in Jenkins, *Papers,* 4:46–47.

100. DeShields, *Tall Men with Long Rifles,* 150.

101. Webb, ed., *Handbook of Texas,* 2:346.

102. Ford, *Fall of the Alamo,* 26.

103. *Catalogue of the Officers and Students of Middlebury College, and Vermont Academy of Medicine,* October 1825, 6.

104. "Testimony of Susanna Hannig, before Sam J. R. McDowell, clerk of the county court, Caldwell, Texas," 6/30/1857, quoted in King, *Susanna Dickinson,* 77.

105. *Ibid.*

106. *Ibid.,* 70. "Statement of Susanna Bellows to notary, J. Castanie, Harris County, Texas," 11/21/1853.

107. *Ibid.*

108. Linda Ericson, "A Frenchman at the Alamo," *Texas Historian* (Summer 1971):15.

109. Blake, "Vindication of Rose," 39.

110. Mrs. S. A. Hannig, statement before Adjutant General of Texas (n.d.), Adjutant General's Miscellaneous Papers, Archives Division, Texas State Library, Austin.

111. *Residents of Texas 1782–1836* (n.p.), The University of Texas Institute of Texan Cultures (n.d.), 198.

112. The Runaway Scrape was the flight of Texan citizens and the retreat of the Texan army before the onslaught of Santa Anna's army, sparked by the fall of the Alamo and the massacre at Goliad. The flight only ended with Houston's defeat of Santa Anna at San Jacinto on 4/21/1836.

113. In September 1842, Mexican General Adrian Woll led a thousand-man force on a reinvasion of Texas. They seized and oc-

cupied San Antonio for a short time, but by September 20 had retreated back into Mexico.

114. William B. Travis to Henry Smith, 1/28/1836, Archives Division, Texas State Library, Austin.

115. Statement of Col. James C. Neill, 9/30/1837, cited in Curtis, *Remember the Alamo Heroes*, 57.

116. Curtis, *Remember the Alamo Heroes*, 57.

117. Launcelot Smither to Stephen F. Austin, 11/4/1835, printed in Jenkins, *Papers*, 2:318–19.

118. Sutherland, "The Fall of the Alamo," in DeShields, *Tall Men with Long Rifles*, 153.

119. David G. Burnet was the first president of the Republic of Texas, elected by the Convention of Texas in March 1836.

120. Curtis, *Remember the Alamo Heroes*, 39.

121. William B. Travis to Henry Smith, 1/28 and 1/29/1835, Archives Division, Texas State Library, Austin.

122. Williams, "A Critical Study," 2:84.

123. Asa Walker to W. W. Gant, 11/28/1835, printed in Lord, *A Time to Stand*, 82–83.

124. DRT, *Muster Rolls*, 42.

125. J. M. Morphis, *History of Texas* (New York: United States Publishing Co., 1875), 176.

126. Potter, *The Fall of the Alamo*, 25.

127. Court of Claims Voucher, no. 400, File (S–Z), General Land Office of Texas, Austin, cited in Williams, "A Critical Study," 4:283.

128. Grant Foreman, *Indians and Pioneers: The Story of the American Southwest Before 1830* (Norman, OK: Univ. of Oklahoma Press, 1936), 46–47.

129. Agreement between the captain of the Cherokee Nation and the governor of Texas, 11/8/1822, Nacogdoches Archives, Archives Division, Texas State Library, Austin.

130. Worth S. Ray, *Austin Colony Pioneers* (Austin and New York: Jenkins Publishing Co., 1970), 254.

131. DRT, *Muster Rolls*, 42.

132. Charles W. Evers to unidentified Ohio newspaper, 3/14/1878, printed in *San Antonio Express*, 2/24/1929.

133. Petition by Mary V. Tauzin, 11/18/1841, no. 21. file box no. 88, letter T, Archives Division, Texas State Library, Austin.

134. Sanford C. Gladden, *The Durst and Darst Families of America with Discussions of Some Forty Related Families* (n.p.: 1969), entry concerning Mary V. Durst.

135. Pay authorization of Anthony Wolf, Dec.d by George W. Hockley, 12/19/1841, Archives Division, Texas State Library, Austin.

136. Evers to Ohio newspaper, printed in *San Antonio Express*, 2/24/1929.

137. Statement of Col. J. C. Neill, document no. X28-3, Archives Division, Texas State Library, Austin.

Part II

1. Quote by Mardell Plainfeather. Jordan, "Ghosts," 813.

2. Charles A. Parker, 11/20/1835, *Natchez Courier*, 12/2/1835, printed in Jenkins, *Papers*, 2:475–76.

3. Goodrich to Houston, 11/28/1835.

4. Bonham to Houston, 12/1/1835.

5. Micajah Autry to Martha Autry, 12/7/1835, *Quarterly of the Texas State Historical Association* 14, no. 4 (April 1911):317–18.

6. Proceedings and Resolutions of a Texas Meeting, 12/9/1835, typescript in Army Papers, Archives Division, Texas State Library, Austin, printed in Jenkins, *Papers*, 3:130–31.

7. Micajah Autry to Martha Autry, 12/13/1835, *Quarterly of the Texas State Historical Association* 14, no. 4 (April 1911):318–19.

8. John M. Thurston to Sam Houston, 12/18/1835, Archives Division, Texas State Library, Austin.

9. Cloud to Cloud, 12/26/1835.

10. Daniel Cloud, *Jackson Mississippian*, 5/6/1836, copy in Cloud file, DRT Library at the Alamo, San Antonio.

11. David Crockett to daughter, 1/9/1836, printed in Williams, "A Critical Study," 110.

12. Carey to brothers and sister, 1/12/1836.

13. Micajah Autry to Martha Autry, 1/13/1836, *Quarterly of the Texas State Historical Association* 14, no. 4 (April 1911):319–20.

14. John H. Forsyth to Council, 1/13/1836, Memorials and Petitions File, Archives Division, Texas State Library, Austin, printed in Jenkins, *Papers*, 3:504–505.

15. Amos Pollard to Henry Smith, 1/16/1836, Army Papers, Archives Division, Texas State Library, Austin.

16. Although he indicated the northwest corner, Jameson undoubtedly meant the southwest corner, which was the only corner of the Alamo from which an artillery piece could command Bexar, and which is the generally recognized position of the eighteen-pounder.

17. Green B. Jameson to Sam Houston, 1/18/1836, printed in de Zavala, *The Alamo*, 18–20.

18. Court of Claims Vouchers, no. 4271, File A–C, General Land Office of Texas, printed in Jenkins, *Papers*, 4:86–87.

19. Joseph M. Hawkins to Henry Smith, 1/20/1836, Army Papers, Archives Division, Texas State Library, Austin, printed in Jenkins, *Papers,* 4:88.

20. William B. Travis to W. G. Hill, 1/21/1836, Ruby Mixon, "William Barret Travis: His Life and Letters" (M.A. thesis, University of Texas at Austin, 1930), 432; printed in Jenkins, *Papers,* 109.

21. Joseph M. Hawkins to James Robinson, 1/24/1836, printed in Curtis, *Remember the Alamo Heroes,* 18–19.

22. Amos Pollard to Henry Smith, 1/27/1836, Army Papers, Archives Division, Texas State Library, Austin.

23. William B. Travis to Henry Smith, 1/28/1836, State Department Record Books, Archives Division, Texas State Library, Austin.

24. William B. Travis to Henry Smith, 1/29/1836, Army Papers, Archives Division, Texas State Library, Austin.

25. James Bowie to Henry Smith, 2/21/1835 [1836], Army Papers, Archives Division, Texas State Library, Austin, printed in Jenkins, *Papers,* 4:236–38.

26. It was the belief of several of the Alamo's officers that Colonel Neill left Bexar due to illness in his family. This may or may not have been the case. When he left Bexar, it was with every intention of returning. Neill placed Travis in command temporarily, pending his return. On 2/28/1836 Neill was in San Felipe and received $600 from Governor Henry Smith for the use of the troops at Bexar. It can only be assumed that the chaotic events in Texas, lack of sufficient troops, and the extent of the Mexican siege at the Alamo prevented Neill's return. Over the years, Neill has been increasingly viewed with the unjust and untrue attitude that he simply abandoned his post at Bexar or that he was nudged aside by more competant officers.

27. Green B. Jameson to Henry Smith, 2/11/1836, Army Papers, Archives Division, Texas State Library, Austin, printed in Jenkins, *Papers,* 4:303.

28. William B. Travis to Henry Smith, 2/12/1836, Army Papers, Archives Division, Texas State Library, Austin, printed in Jenkins, *Papers,* 4:317–18.

29. Baugh to Smith, 2/13/1836.

30. Travis to Smith, 2/13/1836.

31. Amos Pollard to Henry Smith, 2/13/1836, Consultation Papers, Archives Division, Texas State Library, Austin.

32. David P. Cummings to his father, 2/14/1836, Court of Claims Vouchers, no. 4271. File A–C, Texas General Land Office, Austin, printed in Jenkins, *Papers,* 4:333–35.

33. William B. Travis and James Bowie to Henry Smith, 2/14/

1835 [1836], Texas Collection, Bancroft Library, University of California, Berkeley, printed in Jenkins, *Papers,* 4:339.

34. Green B. Jameson to Henry Smith, 2/16/1836, Consultation Papers, Archives Division, Texas State Library, Austin, printed in Jenkins, *Papers,* 4:352–53.

35. William B. Travis to Andrew Ponton, 2/23/1836, Streeter Collection, Yale University Library, New Haven, printed in Jenkins, *Papers,* 4:420.

36. William B. Travis to the People of Texas, 2/24/1836, Archives Division, Texas State Library, Austin, printed in Jenkins, *Papers,* 4:423.

37. Launcelot Smither to All the Inhabitants of Texas, 2/24/1836, Army Papers, Archives Division, Texas State Library, Austin, printed in Jenkins, *Papers,* 4:422.

38. Albert Martin to the People of Texas, 2/25/1836, Davidson Collection, Archives Division, Texas State Library, Austin. This note was added as a postscript to Travis's letter of 2/24/1836. See Green, "To the People of Texas," 493–500.

39. Launcelot Smither postscript to letter by Travis of 2/24/1836, in Jenkins, *Papers,* 4:493–504.

40. Travis to Houston, 2/25/1836.

41. Philip Dimitt to James Kerr, 2/28/1836, Army Papers, Archives Division, Texas State Archives, Austin, printed in Jenkins, *Papers,* 4:453.

42. William B. Travis to [Jesse Grimes], 3/3/1836, *Telegraph and Texas Register,* 3/24/1836, photocopy in Archives Division, Texas State Library, Austin.

43. William B. Travis to Texan Convention, 3/3/1836, *Texas Telegraph and Register,* 3/12/1836, printed in Jenkins, *Papers,* 4:502–504.

44. William B. Travis to [David Ayers], 3/3/1836, *Texas Monument,* 3/31/1852, printed in Jenkins, *Papers,* 4:501.

45. Juan N. Seguin, 2/25/1836, printed in Daughters of the Republic of Texas, *The Alamo — Long Barrack Museum* (Dallas: Taylor Publishing Co., 1986), 43.

46. Esparza, "Alamo's Only Survivor," 5/12 and 5/19/1907.

Selected Bibliography

Published Sources

Articles

Alexander, J. C. "Massacre at Camp Grant." In *The American West*, ed. Raymond Friday Locke, 39–60. Los Angeles: Mankind Publishing Co., 1971. (Concerning William S. Oury.)

Andersen, Kaj. "Charles Zanco — Alamo Defender and Painter of the Lone Star." *Alamo Lore and Myth Organization Newsletter*, no. 4 (December 1979):3.

Barker, Eugene C. "The Texan Revolutionary Army." *Quarterly of the Texas State Historical Association* 9, no. 4 (April 1906): 227–61.

Bennet, Miles S. "The Battle of Gonzales, The Lexington of the Texas Revolution." *Quarterly of the Texas State Historical Association* 2 (July 1898–April 1899):313–16.

Crimmins, M. L. "John W. Smith, Last Messenger from the Alamo." *Southwestern Historical Quarterly* 54 (1950–51):344–46.

Davis, Curtis Carroll. "A Legend at Full Length — Mr. Chapman Paints Colonel Crockett — And Tells About It." *American Antiquarian Society Proceedings* 69, part 2 (October 1959):155–74.

Drake, David. "Joe, Alamo Hero." *Negro History Bulletin* (April-May-June 1981).

Ericson, Linda. "A Frenchman at the Alamo." *Texas Historian* (1971):10–15

Funk, Arville. "A Hoosier at the Alamo." *Alamo Lore and Myth Organization Newsletter* 4, no. 1 (1982):14–16.

Green, Michael R. "To the People of Texas and All Americans in the World." *Southwestern Historical Quarterly* 91, no. 4 (April 1988):483–508.

Groneman, Bill. "Charles Zanco — Alamo Hero." *American Dane Magazine* 69, no. 8 (August 1985):6.

———. "Anthony Wolf — Tracing an Alamo Defender." *Journal of South Texas* 3, no. 1 (Spring 1990):24–35.

179

————. "Lewis Dewall (Duel)." *The Alamo News: Newsletter of Alamo International,* no. 40 (May 1984):5–10.

Ivey, Jake. "The Losoyas and the Texas Revolution." *Alamo Lore and Myth Organization Newsletter* 4, no. 1 (March 1982):12–13.

————. "The Problem of the Two Guerreros." *Alamo Lore and Myth Organization Newsletter* 4, no. 1 (March 1982): 10–12.

Jordan, Robert P. "Ghosts on the Little Bighorn." *National Geographic Magazine* 170, no. 6 (December 1986):813.

Joyce, William L. "Rhode Island's Alamo Hero." *American Legion Magazine* (June 1977):19.

Kellman, Steven G. "The Yellow Rose of Texas." *Journal of American Culture* 2 (Summer 1982):45–48.

Lindley, Thomas R. "Alamo Sources." *Alamo Journal,* no. 74 (December 1990).

Looscan, Adele B. "Micajah Autry, A Soldier of the Alamo." *Quarterly of the Texas State Historical Association* 14, no. 4 (April 1911):315–24.

Malkowski, Karen. "New Hero of the Alamo Discovered." *San Antonio Express News,* 9/13/1986, 1-C.

McCall, G. A. "William T. Malone." *Quarterly of the Texas State Historical Association* 14, no. 4 (April 1911):325–27.

Miller, Thomas L. "Mexican-Texans at the Alamo." *Journal of Mexican-American History* 2, no. 1 (Fall 1973):33–44.

Pittman, Ruth. "One Did Survive." *Elks Club Magazine* (May 1982).

Rather, Ethel Z. "DeWitt's Colony." *Quarterly of the Texas State Historical Association* 8, no. 2 (October 1904):95–191.

Sibley, Marilyn McAdams. "The Burial Place of Alamo Heroes." *Southwestern Historical Quarterly* 70 (1966–67):272–280.

Voss, Frederick S. "Portraying an American Original: The Likenesses of Davy Crockett." *Southwestern Historical Quarterly* 91, no. 4 (April 1988):457–82.

Williams, Amelia M. "A Critical Study of the Siege of the Alamo and of the Personnel of Its Defenders." Ph.D. diss., University of Texas, 1931. Published in abridged form, *Southwestern Historical Quarterly* 36 and 37 (1933–1934).

————. "Notes on Alamo Survivors." *Southwestern Historical Quarterly* 49 (1946):634–37.

Winston, James E. "New York and the Independence of Texas." *Southwestern Historical Quarterly* 18 (1915):368–85.

Young, Kevin. "Dimmitt's 1824 Flag." *Alamo Journal* 53 (December 1986): 10–12.

Books

Abstract of the Original Titles of Record in the General Land Office. Houston: National Banner Office — Niles & Co., 1838. Reprint. Austin: Pemberton Press, 1964.

Boatright, Mody C., and Donald Day, eds. *From Hell to Breakfast.* Austin: Texas Folklore Society, 1944. Reprint. Dallas: Southern Methodist University Press, 1967.

Branda, Eldon Stephen, ed. *The Handbook of Texas: A Supplement.* Vol. 3. Austin: Texas State Historical Assc., 1976.

Catalogue of the Officers and Students of Middlebury College and Vermont Academy of Medicine. Castletown, VT: privately published, 1825.

Chabot, Frederick C. *With the Makers of San Antonio.* San Antonio: privately published, 1937.

Curtis, Albert. *Remember the Alamo Heroes.* San Antonio: Clegg Co., 1961.

Daughters of the Republic of Texas. *The Alamo Heroes and Their Revolutionary Ancestors.* San Antonio: privately published, 1976.

———. *The Alamo — Long Barrack Museum.* Dallas: Taylor Publishing Co., 1986.

———. *Founders and Patriots of the Republic of Texas.* Austin: privately published, 1963.

———. *Muster Rolls of the Texas Revolution.* Austin: privately published, 1986.

Davis, Robert E., ed. *Diary of William Barret Travis, Aug. 30, 1833–June 26, 1834.* Waco, Texas: Texian Press, 1966.

DeShields, James T. *Tall Men with Long Rifles.* San Antonio: Naylor Co., 1935. Reprint. 1971.

DeZavala, Adina. *The Alamo — Where the Last Man Died.* San Antonio: Naylor Co., 1956.

Dobie, J. Frank, Mody C. Boatright, and Harry H. Ransom, eds. *In the Shadow of History.* Austin: Texas Folklore Society, 1939. Reprint. Detroit: Folklore Associates, 1971.

Ericson, Carolyn R. *Citizens and Foreigners of the Nacogdoches District 1809–1836.* Nacogdoches, Texas: Ericson Books, 1981.

Ferris, Sylvia Van Voast, and Eleanor Sellers Hoppe. *Scalpels and Sabers.* Austin: Eakin Press, 1985.

Ford, John S. *Origin and Fall of the Alamo.* San Antonio: Johnson Brothers Printing Co., 1900. Reprint. Austin: Shelby Publishers, 1980.

Gray, William Fairfax. *From Virginia to Texas, 1835–36.* Houston: Gray, Dillaye & Co., 1909. Reprint. Houston: Fletcher Young Publishing Co., 1965.

Hauck, Richard Boyd. *Crockett: A Bio-Bibliography*. Westport, CT: Greenwood Press, 1982.

Jenkins, John H., ed. *Papers of the Texas Revolution 1835–1836*. 10 vols. Austin: Presidial Press, 1973.

King, C. Richard. *Susanna Dickinson — Messenger of the Alamo*. Austin: Shoal Creek Publishers, 1976.

Lord, Walter. *A Time to Stand*. New York: Harper & Row Publishers, 1961.

Maverick, Mary A., and George M. Maverick. *Memoirs of Mary A. Maverick*. San Antonio: Alamo Printing Co., 1921.

Morphis, J. M. *History of Texas*. New York: United States Publishing Co., 1875.

Mullins, Marion Day. *First Census of Texas 1829–1836*. Special Publications no. 22. Washington, DC: National Genealogical Society, 1982.

Myers, John Myers. *The Alamo*. New York: E.P. Dutton & Co., 1948.

Nance, Joseph Milton. *Attack and Counter Attack*. Austin: University of Texas Press, 1964.

Nevin, David. *The Texans*. The Old West Series. New York: Time-Life Books, 1975.

Newell, Chester. *History of the Revolution in Texas*. New York: Wiley & Putnam, 1838. Reprint. Far Western Frontier Series. New York: Arno Press, 1973.

Nixon, Pat I. *Medical Story of Early Texas 1582–1853*. San Antonio: Mollie Bennett Lupe Memorial Fund, 1946.

Perry Carmen, ed. and trans. *With Santa Anna in Texas*. College Station, TX: Texas A&M University Press, 1975.

Potter, Reuben M. "Fall of the Alamo." *Magazine of American History* (January 1878). Reprint (in book form). Hillsdale, NJ: Otterden Press, 1977.

Ray, Worth S. *Austin Colony Pioneers*. Austin and New York: Pemberton Press, Jenkins Publishing Co., 1970.

Record of Southwest Texas. Chicago: Goodspeed Brothers Publishers, 1894.

Residents of Texas 1782–1836. Vol. 2. N.p.: University of Texas Institute of Texan Cultures, n.d.

Rosenthal, Phil, and Bill Groneman. *Roll Call at the Alamo*. Vol. 1, Source Texana Series. Fort Collins, CO: Old Army Press, 1986.

Shackford, James A. *David Crockett: the Man and the Legend*. Chapel Hill, NC: University of North Carolina Press, 1956. Reprint. Westport, CT: Greenwood Press, 1981.

Sowell, A. J. *Early Settlers and Indian Fighters of Southwest Texas*. Austin: Ben C. Jones & Co., 1900. Reprint. Austin: State House Press, 1986.

———. Rangers and Pioneers of Texas. San Antonio: 1884. Reprint. New York: Argosy — AntiQuarian Ltd., 1964.

Webb, Walter Prescott, et al., eds. *Handbook of Texas*. Vols. 1 and 2. Austin: Texas State Historical Assc., 1952.

White, Clifford. *1830 Citizens of Texas*. Austin: Eakin Publications Inc., 1983.

Wright, S. J. *San Antonio de Bexar*. Austin: Morgan Printing Co., 1916.

Newspapers

Esparza, Enrique. "Alamo's Only Survivor." Interview by Charles Merritt Barnes. *San Antonio Express*, 5/12 and 5/19/1907.

Evers, Charles W. "Survived the Alamo Massacre." *San Antonio Express*, 2/24/1929.

Gray, William F. "Letter From Texas." *Frankfort (Kentucky) Commonwealth*, 5/25/1836, p. 2.

San Antonio Express, 12/21/1917. (Obituary of Enrique Esparza.)

San Antonio Light, 12/21/1917. (Obituary of Enrique Esparza.)

"Survivor of the Alamo." *San Antonio Daily Express*, 4/28/1881.

Telegraph and Texas Register, 3/24/1836.

Velazques de Leon, Juan L. "Traduccion de una Carta de R.M. Willianson [*sic*] al Cabecilla Barret Travis." *El Nacional* (Mexico City) suplemento al numero 79, 3/21/1836.

Unpublished Material

Archival Material

Abstract of Land Titles of Erath County, Texas. (Concerning William Howell.)

Application Papers of Walker Baylor to the U.S. Military Academy at West Point, 8, 2/25/1831, 1/19/1832. Archives, U.S. Military Academy, West Point, New York.

Hannig, S. A. "Statement of Mrs. S. A. Hannig Wife of Almaron Dic[k]enson (Or Dickerson)." Adjutant General's Miscellaneous Papers, Archives Division, Texas State Library, Austin.

Hannig, Susanna. "Testimony of Mrs. Hannig touching the Alamo Massacre. 23 September 1876." Archives Division, Texas State Library, Austin.

Holdings of the Daughters of the Republic of Texas Library at the Alamo, San Antonio. (Concerning: James L. Allen; Juana Navarro de Alsbury; John W. Baylor; Daniel Bourne; Daniel W. Cloud; Francis DeSauque; Lewis Dewall; Susannah Dickerson; Esparza Family; James C. Neill; Juan N. Seguin; Launcelot Smither; Andrew J. Sowell; and Anthony Wolf.)

Holdings of the Texas General Land Office, Austin. (Concerning: Gregorio Esparza; and Damacio Ximenes.)

Republic of Texas Records, Texas State Archives. (Concerning: James L. Allen; John W. Baylor; Daniel Bourne; James Bowie; William R. Carey; Lemuel Crawford; Francis DeSauque; Susannah Dickerson; John H. Forsyth; Benjamin F. Nobles; Amos Pollard; John M. Thurston; William B. Travis; Anthony Wolf; and Charles Zanco.)

Travis Papers 1831–1924. Library of the University of Texas at Austin.

Correspondence

Andersen, Kaj, Copenhagen, to Bill Groneman, New York. 1/1, 2/9, 3/7, and 7/22/1984. Copies in files of author. (Concerning Charles Zanco.)

Esparza, Ray, San Antonio, to Bill Groneman, New York. 8/14/1988. Copy in files of author. (Concerning the Esparza family.)

Haythornthwaite, Philip, England, to Kevin Young, Texas. 2/2 and 2/19/1983. Copies in files of author. (Concerning Louis Rose.)

Holley, Mrs. Mary Austin, Mobile, Alabama, to Mrs. W. Brand, Lexington, Kentucky, 3/24/1837. Barker Texas History Center, University of Texas, Austin. (Concerning John W. Baylor.)

Lefler, James, to Etna Scott, 9/23/1983. Copy in files of author. (Concerning Maria Josefa Ana Estacia Esparza.)

Scott, Etna, to James Lefler, 11/12/1983. Copy in files of author. (Concerning Maria Josefa Ana Estacia Esparza.)

Ximenes, Ben, to Marjorie Clapp, *San Antonio Light*. San Antonio, n.d. Copy in files of author. (Concerning Damacio Ximenes.)

Young, Kevin, Texas, to Philip Haythornthwaite and Tom Devoe, n.d. Copy in files of author. (Concerning Louis Rose.)

Genealogical

Esparza, Reynaldo J. "Family Tree of José Frederico Esparza." n.d. Copy in Gregorio Esparza File, DRT Library at the Alamo, San Antonio.

Family Tree of John Crossman or Crosman of Somerset, England.

Copy in private collection of Clifford Choquette, Chelmsford, Massachusetts.

Gladden, Sanford Charles. *The Durst and Darst Families of America with Discussions of Some Forty Related Families.* N.p: privately printed, 1969. (Concerning Anthony Wolf.)

McMurtry, Zelma M. *William Glass of Virginia and Kentucky and His Descendants of Scott and Owen Counties, Kentucky.* Lexington, KY: privately printed, 1975. (Concerning Daniel Bourne.)

Williams, Grover B. "Daniel Bourne." Daniel Bourne File. DRT Library at the Alamo, San Antonio.

Manuscripts

Choquette, Clifford J., and Marcelle R. Choquette. "Ashburnham to the Alamo, Amos Pollard, M.D." Chelmsford, MA: 1981.

Groneman, Bill. "Research Material for *Roll Call at the Alamo*." A Lorimar Pictures mini-series intended for television. Howard Beach, NY: 1985.

"Lost Book of Harris." Copied by Gifford White from the original in the Texas General Land Office. Austin: 1968.

Scott, Etna. "Information — Enrique Esparza, 6 February 1984." Gregorio Esparza File. DRT Library at the Alamo, San Antonio.

Seguin, Juan N. "Personal Memoirs of Juan N. Seguin, 1858." Typescript copy in the Juan N. Seguin File. DRT Library at the Alamo, San Antonio.

Smith, Col. William O. "Life of William Sander Oury 1817–1887." 1930. Barker Texas History Center, University of Texas, Austin.

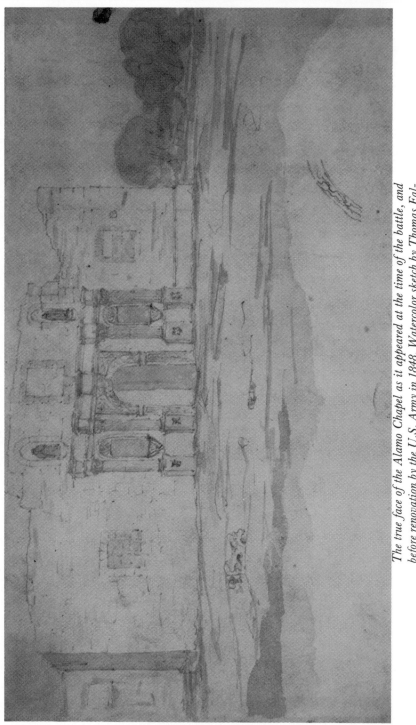

The true face of the Alamo Chapel as it appeared at the time of the battle, and before renovation by the U.S. Army in 1848. Watercolor sketch by Thomas Falconer, 1841.

— Courtesy Western American Collection,
Beinecke Rare Book and Manuscript Library,
Yale University

W.B. Travis
By Wiley Martin
Dec. 1835

William Barret Travis, commander of the Alamo garrison. Sketch by Wiley Martin, 1835.

— Courtesy, DeGolyer Library, Southern Methodist University, Dallas, Texas

James Bowie, commander of the volunteer troops among the Alamo garrison. From a portrait by George P. A. Healy, ca. 1831–34.

— Courtesy Archives Division, Texas State Library

David Crockett, former United States congressman from the state of Tennessee, in one of several portraits done from life. Watercolor on paper by James H. Shegogue, 1831.

— Courtesy National Portrait Gallery, Smithsonian Institution, Washington, D.C.

Juan N. Seguin, highest-ranking officer to leave the Alamo as a courier. He was returning with reinforcements when the Alamo fell. Portrait by Thomas Jefferson Wright, 1838.

— Courtesy Archives Division, Texas State Library

Amos Pollard, M.D., chief surgeon of the Alamo garrison.
— Courtesy Archives Division, Texas State Library

Susannah Dickerson, wife of Alamo defender, Almeron Dickerson. Photo taken years after the Alamo battle.

— Courtesy Archives Division, Texas State Library

Angelina Dickerson, daughter of Almeron and Susannah Dickerson, a child survivor of the Alamo battle. Photo taken years after the Alamo battle.
— Courtesy Prints and Photographs Collection, Barker Texas History Center, University of Texas at Austin

Dr. John Sutherland. An injured knee saved him from the Alamo massacre.
Photo taken years after the Alamo battle.

Benjamin F. Highsmith, an Alamo courier. Photo taken years after the Alamo battle.

— From *Early Settlers and Indian Fighters of Southwest Texas* by A. J. Sowell

William S. Oury, an Alamo courier. Photo taken years after the Alamo battle.
— Courtesy Arizona Historical Society

Enrique Esparza, child survivor of the Alamo battle. Neither age nor infirmity would make him forget. Photo ca. 1907.